A Toolkit *for* Confessions

Recovering *our* Confessional Heritage #4

Recovering *our* Confessional Heritage

James M. Renihan, Editor-in-Chief
Richard C. Barcellos, Managing Editor

James M. Renihan, *Associational Churchmanship: Second London Confession of Faith 26.12-15*
Richard C. Barcellos, *The Covenant of Works: Its Confessional and Scriptural Basis*
James M. Renihan, *A Toolkit for Confessions: Symbolics 101 – Helps for the Study of English Puritan Confessions of Faith*

A Toolkit for Confessions

Symbolics 101

— Helps for the Study of English Puritan Confessions of Faith —

James M. Renihan

The Institute of Reformed Baptist Studies
Printed by RBAP, Palmdale, CA

Copyright © 2017 James M. Renihan. All rights reserved.

Requests for information should be sent to:

RBAP
349 Sunrise Terrace
Palmdale, CA 93551
rb@rbap.net
www.rbap.net

No part of this publication may be reproduced, stored in a retrieval system, or transmitted in any way by any means, electronic, mechanical, photocopy, recording, or otherwise, without the prior permission of RBAP except as provided by USA copyright law.

Printed in the United States of America.

Cover design and formatted for print by Cameron Porter. Front cover Confession text was captured and graphically modified from document excerpts at Columbia University Libraries: https://clio.columbia.edu/catalog/4540105.

ISBN-13: 978-0-9965198-1-6

Endorsements

I first heard Jim Renihan speak on the Second London Confession of Faith at a conference in Charlesworth, Derbyshire, several years ago and I immediately warmed to him because he clearly loved my country, my heritage, and my forefathers in the faith. At the same time I was ashamed that I knew so little about these men and that my understanding of their system of theology was so limited. Having lived for years on a restricted diet of "Biblical Theology," I realized that my preaching had become lopsided and despite following the consecutive expository method, I had unwittingly been neglecting and even misrepresenting major doctrines in my ministry.

Through hearing and meditating upon the material now made available in this very helpful little book, I have come to value the system of doctrine laid out in the Confession. As a church we have enjoyed its breadth and depth and found a new confidence in our faith. Through studying the Confession together, with the help of Dr. Renihan's "Toolkit," we have come to enjoy a new strength of unity and depth of joy in "the faith that was once for all delivered to the saints." Our great desire now is to preserve and pass on this faith to the coming generation.

Oliver Allmand-Smith
Pastor
Trinity Grace Church
Lancashire, UK

****

Many pastors and elders serve churches that formally subscribe the 1689 Second London Confession of Faith but are only vaguely aware of the document's historical context. Much of the problem stems from a lack of reliable and accessible materials that treat Baptist contributions to seventeenth-century ecclesiastical history. Baptist church leaders must often make do with historical and theological analyses of the Westminster standards, adapting them to their own context as best they can. James Renihan's *A Toolkit for Confessions* represents a major step toward remedying this need. By combining historical and theological insight into the Second London Confession with a primer on reading early modern confessions more generally, this book represents a unique resource that should become a standard point of departure for confessional Reformed Baptist churches seeking to explore their theological heritage. *A Toolkit for Confessions* will be tremendously helpful to anyone who wishes to better understand both the Second London Confession itself and the ecclesiastical context out of which it emerged.

Dr. Matthew C. Bingham
Queen's University Belfast
Belfast, UK

****

The Second London Confession is a biblical and beautiful articulation of the Christian faith that has served Baptists well for well over 300 years. But it is also an old document that emerged in a time very different from our own, which leaves many modern readers sometimes confused. *A Toolkit for Confessions* is a welcome and necessary resource for those who want to understand and use the Second London in the local church or even in their personal lives. In this small and accessible work, Dr. Renihan effectively educates and equips the reader to get much more from the Confession than would be possible without it. By shedding light on the purpose, structure, language, and doctrinal emphases of the Second London Confession this "toolkit" becomes an essential companion to our beloved Confession of Faith, and a must for every Baptist library.

Joe Thorn
Author and Lead Pastor
Redeemer Fellowship
St. Charles, IL

****

When we first arrive at a destination like a famous museum or cathedral it is easy to be overwhelmed. We may look for a guide who will be able to help us understand the background, history, and significance of the place. Our best guides both inform our minds and engage our attention. When we come to the Second London Confession of Faith, we may be grateful to have just such a guide in James M. Renihan's *A Toolkit for Confessions*. Renihan provides us an accessible and instructive introduction to the background, history, context, structure, and contents of the 2LCF. Baptist readers will especially benefit from this study of an important but often neglected part of the Baptist confessional and theological heritage. Baptist and non-Baptist readers alike will appreciate the ways in which Renihan shows how the 2LCF constructively relates to the broader family of Reformed confessions. *A Toolkit for Confessions* is a welcome and valuable addition to the growing body of literature on the confessions and catechisms of the seventeenth century.

Guy Prentiss Waters, Ph.D
James M. Baird, Jr. Professor of New Testament
Reformed Theological Seminary
Jackson, MS

****

Table of Contents

Series Preface 1
Acknowledgements 5
1. Introduction 7
2. Background Reading 19
3. The Text of the Confession 25
4. The Words of the Confession 31
5. The Puritan Confessional Context 41
6. Important Helps 53
7. How the Confession is Organized 63
8. The Doctrinal Emphases of the
   Confession 85
9. Editorial Principles 93
10. The Baptist Catechism 99
11. Conclusion: John Owen on
    Confessionalism 109
Appendix 115
For Reading and Reference 119

Series Preface

The purpose of the series *Recovering our Confessional Heritage* is to address issues related to the Second London Confession of Faith of 1677/89 (2LCF). This centuries-old Confession is widely recognized as the most important Confession of Faith in Baptist history. First published in England in 1677, it became the standard for Baptists in Colonial America through the publication of the Philadelphia (1742), Ketockton, Virginia (1766), Charleston, South Carolina, Warren, Rhode Island (both 1767), and many other editions of the Confession. As late as 1881, William Cathcart, the editor of *The Baptist Encyclopedia*, could say, "In England and America, churches, individuals, and Associations, with clear minds, with hearts full of love for the truth, . . . have held with veneration the articles of 1689." Since then, it has been adopted by Baptists around the world and translated into many languages.

We believe that, due to two factors, producing a series of short books on the 2LCF will be useful to many pastors and church members. First, there has been increased interest in the 2LCF in the first decade and a half of the twenty-first century. In fact, from the early 1960s, a greater awareness of this Confession among Baptists in the United States and around the world is evident. One of the encouraging proofs of this growing attention is the multiplication of churches who identify the 2LCF as their confessional standard.

Second, there are many issues related to the Confession that need to be clearly and cogently explained in order for an informed and robust recovery of Baptist confessionalism to continue. While churches and individuals have formally adopted the 2LCF as a standard, it has not always been clear that its contents have been fully or properly understood. As a result, the goal of this series is to aid those considering the 2LCF, as well as those already committed to it, in order to produce or maintain an informed and vigorous Baptist confessionalism.

The series will include treatments of various subjects by multiple authors. The subjects to be covered are those the series editors (along with consultants) determine to be of particular interest in our day. The authors will be those who display ample ability to address the issue under discussion. Some of the installments will be more involved than others due to the nature of the subject addressed and perceived current needs. Many of the contributions will cover foundational aspects of the self-consistent theological system expressed in the Confession. Others will address difficult, often misunderstood, or even denied facets of the doctrinal formulations of the 2LCF. Each installment will have a "For Further Reading" bibliography at the end to encourage further study on the issue discussed.

It is hoped that, by the blessing of God, these brief books will produce a better understanding of "the faith which was once for all delivered to the saints" (Jude 3, NKJV) as well as a clearer and more robust understanding of what it means to confess the 2LCF in the twenty-first century.

James M. Renihan, Editor-in-Chief
Richard C. Barcellos, Managing Editor

October 2016

Acknowledgements

The series *Recovering our Confessional Heritage* is sponsored by the Institute of Reformed Baptist Studies in cooperation with Reformed Baptist Academic Press. The Institute of Reformed Baptist Studies is a graduate theological school which aids churches in preparing men to serve in the Gospel Ministry. For more information please visit *irbsseminary.org*.

Many thanks to Dr. Richard Barcellos for both the idea and implementation of this new series of books. We hope that they will be of great usefulness to many.

This book is a revised and expanded version of an article titled "How will I understand unless someone guides me?: Helps for Understanding our Confession of Faith," published in *Reformed Baptist Theological Review*, IV:1 (January 2007): 43-58 and an address delivered at the General Assembly of the Association of Reformed Baptist Churches of America held at Grace Covenant Church, Gilbert, Arizona, in April 2014. I wish to thank Samuel Renihan for several helpful suggestions.

James M. Renihan
February 2017

1.
Introduction

Now an angel of the Lord spoke to Philip, saying, "Arise and go toward the south along the road which goes down from Jerusalem to Gaza." This is desert. So he arose and went. And behold, a man of Ethiopia, a eunuch of great authority under Candace the queen of the Ethiopians, who had charge of all her treasury, and had come to Jerusalem to worship, was returning. And sitting in his chariot, he was reading Isaiah the prophet. Then the Spirit said to Philip, "Go near and overtake this chariot." So Philip ran to him, and heard him reading the prophet Isaiah, and said, "Do you understand what you are reading?" And he said, "How can I, unless someone guides me?" And he asked Philip to come up and sit with him. The place in the Scripture which he read was this:

He was led as a sheep to the slaughter;
And as a lamb before its shearer is silent,
So He opened not His mouth.
In His humiliation His justice was taken away,
And who will declare His generation?
For His life is taken from the earth.

So the eunuch answered Philip and said, "I ask you, of whom does the prophet say this, of himself or of some other man?" Then Philip opened his mouth, and beginning at this Scripture, preached Jesus to him. Now as they went down the road, they came to some water. And the eunuch said, "See, *here is* water. What hinders me from being baptized?" Then Philip said, "If you believe with all your heart, you may." And he answered and said, "I believe that Jesus Christ is the Son of God." So he commanded the chariot to stand still. And both Philip and the eunuch went down into the water, and he baptized him. Now when they came up out of the water, the Spirit of the Lord caught Philip away, so that the eunuch saw him no more; and he went on his way rejoicing. But Philip was found at Azotus. And passing through, he preached in all the cities till he came to Caesarea. (Acts 8:26-40, NKJV)

Introduction

It must have been a strange experience for Philip to travel from Jerusalem to Gaza, into a desert territory, in order to do the work of God, and perhaps what he encountered was even more surprising. There in a chariot was a wealthy Ethiopian eunuch, studying hard and reading aloud words from the prophet Isaiah! The sight of it all must have seemed utterly incongruous, but the acts of God are often astonishing. Deep in his contemplation, the eunuch could not work out the meaning of the words before him. Did the prophet speak of himself, or of another? Philip knew that this might be the case, and offered his services as an interpreter, so that his new friend might understand that Isaiah (and other authors of Scripture) wrote of Jesus. Philip did what every good minister does, he helped someone understand that which he did not previously comprehend.

Just as the Ethiopian eunuch, a religious man in his own right, needed assistance to grasp what he read in his Isaiah scroll, so also do we need assistance in reading our Confession of Faith. There is no doubt that the eunuch was familiar with much about the Scriptures—Luke tells us that he was returning to Ethiopia from Jerusalem, having traveled there for the purpose of worship. The things of God were foremost in his mind, and yet he did not know the meaning of the vital words he read. Familiarity with words and ideas does not guarantee comprehension. He needed Philip.

As *confessional* Christians, we are convinced that our Confession of Faith summarizes the system of doctrine contained in the Holy Scriptures. We recognize that it is a human product, the fruit of centuries of Bible study and theological formulation, but I wonder if sometimes we forget that it is not a modern document in the strictest sense of the term. In fact, it could easily be argued that it is a late-medieval production, published at the very end of that era, just as the Enlightenment was to overwhelm European intellectual life. For this reason, it must be approached cautiously. If the perspicuous Word of God requires careful contextual study and interpretation, how much more so a document of human formulation? In reality, proper understanding of the Confession requires several things of us — familiarity with theological development throughout the preceding centuries, acquaintance with contemporary theological thought (especially in its Reformed variety), and an unwillingness to import twentieth- or twenty-first-century ideas into its words and phrases. This book is intended to assist the interpreter in doing these things.

Confessions of faith have a long and noble history in the life of Christ's church. In the Old Testament, the words of Deuteronomy 6:4ff. ("Hear O Israel, The LORD our God, the LORD is One . . . ") served as the basic confession for Israel. The New Testament writers affirm this truth (see for example 1 Cor. 8:6) and expand it by speaking of Jesus Christ in his person and work (Phil. 2:5-11 is an instance). Within the young church, however, doctrinal and moral problems arose (consider Paul's epistles to the Corinthians, Galatians, Colossians, etc.). And after the days of the apostles, as the fledgling church grew and spread, it faced similar challenges, both from within its ranks and through errors creeping in from outside. Following the well-established pattern of Scripture, the leaders of the churches wrote creeds and confessions to express in clear and definitive terms the "faith once for all delivered to the saints" (Jude 3).

What is a Confession of Faith?

A confession of faith is an extensive statement of Christian doctrine, carefully expressed in language recognized and understood among Christians throughout the ages. It serves two purposes: first, it ties Christians to the church catholic. One danger that frequently faces the church in its own era might be what C. S. Lewis called "chronological snobbery"[1] — thinking that its faith and practice is the final and essential expression of Christianity. The remedy for this danger is remembering the doctrine of the communion of the saints through the ages. This is vital, in that it recognizes that Christians are part of a body that has confessed the truth about God and Christ for two millennia. Second, a confession expresses the distinctive doctrines of the group publishing it. Though it must incorporate catholic doctrine, at the same time it expresses the distinguishing tenets of its advocates. While Reformed Baptists and Reformed paedobaptists have much in common, they differ, for example, on the matter of baptism. Their respective confessions describe these areas of difference. In these two

---

[1] C. S. Lewis, *Surprised by Joy* (New York: Harcourt, Brace, Jovanovich, 1966), 206ff.

ways, confessions draw boundaries—of inclusion and exclusion. Based carefully on Scripture as it has been understood by believers from the apostolic age until today, it provides an important theological identity to its subscribing churches.

These confessions, traditionally called *symbols*, are of great benefit to churches and believers. The time dedicated to know them as summaries of the most important doctrines is well spent. Since they are called *symbols*, studying them is called *Symbolics*.

The Second London Confession of Faith in Historical Context

This book is intended to help you begin to study an important Confession of Faith. Though we consider specifically the *Second London Confession of Faith* (2LCF—often popularly known as the *1689 Confession*), most of the things we will learn here may be applied to other confessions as well. This is especially true of the major English Confessions, the *Westminster Confession of Faith* (WCF) and the lesser known but still very important *Savoy Declaration of Faith and Platform of Polity* (Savoy).

These two documents provide most of the source material for 2LCF. The first of them is the product of the Westminster Assembly, a body of theologians who were called into existence by the English Parliament in 1643. The WCF is one of the finest statements of Christian faith ever produced, and has had a worldwide influence for the past 350 years. It serves as the basis for 2LCF—it is something of a grandparent. The *Savoy* might be considered the immediate parent of 2LCF. It was published by Congregational theologians who met in London in 1658 at a place known as the Savoy Palace. It was a minor revision of the WCF, incorporating some important ideas omitted from it and adjusting the teaching about the church to fit a Congregational rather than Presbyterian form of church life and practice. In most cases, 2LCF follows the changes to WCF made by Savoy, though it does restore the readings from WCF about eleven times.

The first known literary reference to our Confession of Faith is from the Church Minute Book of the Petty France Church in London. This is the church that Nehemiah Coxe and William Collins served. They were ordained together on the same day in 1675. The book is now at the London Metropolitan Archives in the city of London. The minute in the Church Book says, "It was agreed that a Confession of faith, wth the Appendix thereto having bene read & considered by the Bre: should be published." The note also says, "26 August, 1677."[2] It is thought (and this is a fair conclusion) that the Confession actually came out of the Petty France Church and that Coxe and Collins most likely were the men who edited it.[3]

The title page from one of the first editions of the Confession of Faith states "A Confession of Faith put forth by the elders and brethren of many congregations of Christians, baptized upon profession of their faith, in London and the country," followed by a quotation from John chapter 5. At the bottom we read, "Printed in the year 1677." It is curious that many call our Confession the *1689 Confession*. It was never

---

[2] Petty France Church Minute Book 1675-1727, London Metropolitan Archives CLC/179/MS20228/001B "Memoranda and Minutes of Church Meetings and Membership Lists of the Congregations Successively at Petty France, Westminster; Artillery Lane, Spitalfields; Walbrook; and Turners' Hall, Philpot Lane."

[3] For a discussion of this question, see James M. Renihan, *Edification and Beauty: The Practical Ecclesiology of the English Particular Baptists, 1675-1705* (Milton Keynes, UK: Paternoster, 2008), 22ff.

actually printed, so far as we know, in 1689. There were two editions in 1677, one edition in 1688, and one edition in 1699.

Why do we call it, then, the *1689 Confession*? The reason is there was a General Assembly of churches held in September of 1689 in London, hosted by the Broken Wharf Church, and it was there, at that General Assembly of churches, that the Confession was formally adopted. This familiar statement comes to us from the *Narrative* of that 1689 General Assembly:

> We the Ministers, and Messengers of, and concerned for upwards of, one hundred Baptised Congregations in *England* and *Wales* (denying *Arminianism*), being met together in *London*, from the *3d* of the 7th month[4] to the 11th of the same, 1689 to consider of some things that might be for the Glory of God, and the good of these

---

[4] The seventh month is September. The text says ". . . the seventh month . . ." If you think about it, September is the seventh month. In the seventeenth century, New Year's Day was March 25, making March the first month of the year. Counting from March, you have September (seventh month), October (eight month), November (ninth month), December (tenth month), and January and February would be the eleventh and twelfth months of the year. It was not July, which would be the seventh month to us, but September when this meeting was held.

Congregations, have thought meet (for the satisfaction of all other Christians that differ from us in the point of Baptism) to recommend to their perusal the Confession of our Faith, ... which Confession we own, as containing the Doctrine of our Faith and Practice, and do desire that the Members of our Churches respectively do furnish themselves therewith.[5]

When the messengers from these churches first adopted the Confession of Faith publicly and put their names on it, they did it for the purpose of helping other Christians, especially paedobaptists, to understand what they believed and practiced. Basically, they were saying, "We largely agree with you, except not on baptism; we agree with you in the majority of our doctrines; and we urge our churches and our people to have a copy of this so they might be well-instructed in the things we believe."

---

[5] James Renihan, *Faith and Life for Baptists: The Documents of the London Particular Baptist General Assemblies, 1689-1694* (Palmdale, CA: RBAP, 2016), 42.

2.
Background Reading

At the Institute of Reformed Baptist Studies, we offer a course called Baptist Symbolics. In that course, I spend about 50 hours lecturing on the First and Second London Confessions. The vast majority of the time is devoted to 2LCF. This brief book provides some of the introductory material which I present in the class lectures, especially as it relates to 2LCF.

The course description from our catalog says this:

> This course is designed to be a detailed examination of the London Baptist Confession of 1689, with the language explained, supported, and defended so as to understand what the early Baptists asserted. The purpose is to understand the Confession in its historic setting and its relevance to the present. Historical

comparisons will be made to the Westminster and Savoy Confessions. Other Baptist confessions will be considered as they relate to this document.

Careful study, however, does not just involve lectures. When you teach a class like this, you must have required texts. These books have been carefully selected to explain many important facets of both the text of the Confession and the lectures. Because they are so important, it will help you as a student to have access to them. We are blessed by the fact that there is a growing body of literature to assist us in understanding our Confession of Faith.

The first text is Richard Muller's book, *Dictionary of Latin and Greek Theological Terms*.[1] I like to ask my students the question, "Have you bought your groceries yet this week?" I hope they say no so I can then say, "Go buy Muller first." It is that important. Without question, it's one of the most significant and helpful books for study of our Confession of Faith.

---

[1] Muller, Richard A. *Dictionary of Latin and Greek Theological Terms Drawn Principally from Protestant Scholastic Theology*, Second Edition (Grand Rapids: Baker Academic, 2017).

Background Reading

The English Puritan Confessions are the fruit of the Reformation, and are often classified as documents from an era known as Reformed Scholasticism. Though this phrase sounds dry and academic, it really isn't. It simply refers to both a theological commitment (Reformed) and a method of study (Scholasticism). A very useful text book to begin to study this concept is Willem J. Van Asselt's *Introduction to Reformed Scholasticism*.[2] It is helpful in that it explains the basic ideas and assists the student to understand the historical and theological climate from which the Confessions arose.

A more detailed but enormously rewarding set of books to study is Richard Muller's four volume series *Post Reformation Reformed Dogmatics*.[3] The first volume describes the study of theology, the second is devoted to an explanation of how the theologians of the day understood the nature of Scripture, the third and fourth volumes address the doctrine of God in his being, attributes, and trinitarian

---

[2] Willem J. Van Asselt, *Introduction to Reformed Scholasticism* (Grand Rapids: Reformation Heritage Books, 2011).

[3] Richard A. Muller, *Post-Reformation Reformed Dogmatics: The Rise and Development of Reformed Orthodoxy, ca. 1520 to ca. 1725*, 4 Vols. (Grand Rapids: Baker Academic, 2003).

Background Reading

nature. These books are unmatched for their insight into the foundational principles of all the Reformed Confessions.

Since 2LCF is a Baptist document, it is important to note the progression from Reformation to post-Reformation to credobaptism within that theological trajectory. In order to do this, I have my students read my book, *Edification and Beauty*, which is an examination of the doctrine of the church of our fathers, the seventeenth-century English Particular Baptists, as they put this into practice from the Confession of Faith. Another helpful resource is *True Confessions: Baptist Documents in the Reformed Family*.[4] In four sections it places the texts of the two London Confessions, the *Baptist Catechism*, and the *Orthodox Catechism* in columns parallel to their source documents. This makes it simple to see how the Baptist documents relate to other English Puritan confessions and catechisms. Then, of course, we use Dr. Waldron's *A Modern Exposition of the 1689 Baptist Confession of Faith*,[5] urging the

---

[4] James M. Renihan, *True Confessions: Baptist Documents in the Reformed Family* (Owensboro, KY: RBAP, 2004).

[5] Samuel E. Waldron, *A Modern Exposition of the 1689 Baptist Confession of Faith* (Darlington, UK: Evangelical

students to read the appropriate chapters prior to the lectures.

In 2014, John V. Fesko published *The Theology of the Westminster Standards: Historical Context and Theological Insights*.[6] It is an excellent survey of the key doctrines of WCF, and very helpful for the study of our Confession. When supplemented by Chad Van Dixhoorn's recent *Confessing the Faith: A reader's guide to the Westminster Confession of Faith*,[7] there is great help in interpreting the Confession.

I also require my students to obtain a copy of the Westminster Standards in their original, non-American revised form. In 1789, the American Presbyterians revised WCF to meet the recently adopted political circumstances of the new country in which they found themselves. Prior to 1789, WCF required a national church, but the formation of the United States of America explicitly prevented the possibility of a national church, and so the

---

Press, 1989). A fifth revised edition has been published in 2016.

[6] J. V. Fesko, *The Theology of the Westminster Standards: Historical Context and Theological Insights* (Wheaton, IL: Crossway, 2014).

[7] Chad Van Dixhoorn, *Confessing the Faith: A reader's guide to the Westminster Confession of Faith* (Edinburgh; Carlisle, PA: The Banner of Truth Trust, 2014).

majority of American Presbyterians changed their Confession of Faith.

Background Reading

3.
The Text of the Confession

We must begin with the text of the Confession itself, for this is the object of our interest. Some interesting issues arise here. In America, the Confession was published in 1742 (by Benjamin Franklin) with the approval of the Philadelphia Baptist Association. This edition is known as the *Philadelphia Confession* and includes two additional chapters, one on singing in worship and the other on laying on of hands. It was soon after adopted by other Baptist Associations such as Charleston, SC, and Warren, RI. Sometimes modern printers have reprinted these confessions as if they are identical to 2LCF, even though they are not.

Until 1855, editions printed as the *London Baptist Confession* are consistent, but in that year C. H. Spurgeon issued a version with subtle changes, and some modern editions include Spurgeon's alterations—probably without realizing the differences. Two examples may be produced. Most famously, many have wondered how the beginning of chapter 10, paragraph 3, should read. Should the text say "Infants dying in infancy" or "**Elect** infants dying in infancy"? Editions vary—the original includes the word "elect." Spurgeon dropped it. Secondly, some editions differ over the text of chapter 19, paragraph 4. When it speaks of judicial laws, should the text read that their general equity is of "moral" use, or as some read, of "modern" use? The sense is different. "Moral" is the proper reading. Modern editions may differ and the careful student should recognize this fact.

Since there are many different printings of the text itself, the careful student should use some caution when choosing the edition for close study. Three options are readily to be had. The optimum for us all would be to obtain an original seventeenth-century copy. The cost and availability is prohibitive. But the next best case is much simpler: a facsimile of one of the two 1677 editions has recently been printed.[1] This

---

[1] *A Confession of Faith. Put forth by the Elders and Brethren of many Congregations of Christians (baptized upon*

edition provides an immediately accessible reproduction of the text of the Confession as published in the seventeenth century. As a bonus, this version is complete—it includes both the epistle *To the Judicious and Impartial Reader* as well as the *Appendix*. These two pieces ought to be published alongside of the document itself. Sadly, they are seldom available to the student.

The second option involves the purchase of a book that ought to be on every pastor's shelf: William Lumpkin's *Baptist Confessions of Faith*.[2] It is a treasure chest of important Baptist documents, and includes the epistle and the entirety of the Confession, carefully checked against the seventeenth-century versions. Sadly, the *Appendix* is omitted. Despite this, it is an accurate copy and useful for careful and close study.

Perhaps simplest to obtain is the version published by Solid Ground Christian Books under the title *The Baptist Confession of Faith & The Baptist Catechism*. This leather-bound

---

Profession of their Faith) in London and the Country (Auburn, MA: B&R Press, 2000).

[2] William Lumpkin, *Baptist Confessions of Faith* (Valley Forge, PA: Judson Press, 1959, Revised Edition 1959).

edition contains the text of 2LCF itself along with the epistle and appendix.[3]

Another comment should be made. While modern paraphrases can be useful, they are not appropriate for careful study, and should not be the text adopted by a church as its doctrinal statement. The most commonly found modern edition is *A Faith to Confess*.[4] It is certainly beneficial for church members as a helpful and more accessible summary of the doctrines of the Confession, but it should be used with caution. It is not in all places a reliable rendering of the sense of the original document. One might consider the very first sentence of chapter 1, a statement added by the Baptists. The earliest editions read: "The Holy Scripture is the only sufficient, certain, and infallible rule of all

---

[3] *The Baptist Confession of Faith & The Baptist Catechism* (Birmingham, AL: Solid Ground Christian Books, 2010, 2014). There is at least one minor error in the *Appendix* (71). The first sentence should be "Whosoever reads, and impartially considers what we have in our forgoing confession declared, may readily perceive, That we do not only concenter with all other true Christians . . ." The reprint has "consent" rather than "concenter." "That" is capitalized in the original.

[4] *A Faith To Confess: The Baptist Confession of Faith of 1689 Rewritten in Modern English* (Haywards Heath, UK: Carey Publications, 1975). I have seen at least two other modern attempts at paraphrase of 2LCF.

saving knowledge, faith and obedience."[5] The Carey Publications paraphrase, however, renders this as "The Holy Scripture is the all-sufficient, certain and infallible rule or standard of the knowledge, faith and obedience that constitute salvation." The important adverb "only" is eliminated, potentially compromising the exclusive place of Scripture as the *only* sufficient, *only* certain and *only* infallible rule (only is distributive here); "all-sufficient" in itself does not highlight the unique nature of the Word of God, and leaves room for the possibility that there are other writings that might share its characteristics. Paraphrasing is a difficult task, and it leads us to our next item for consideration.

---

[5] *A Confession of Faith*, 1.

4.
The Words of the Confession

All interpretation is, to one degree or another, a paraphrase. We seek to take a text, understand it, and communicate it to others. To do this properly, we must begin with the words contained in the document itself. They are the products of long and careful theological research and reflection, but they are also time-bound. One expects that contemporary readers would have easily comprehended the language but, as each decade passes and the time distance between the reader and the authors increases, great caution must be exercised in seeking to understand the sense of the individual words employed, both as discrete lexemes and in their various contexts.

This is very simple to illustrate. When, for example, chapter 5 paragraph 2 states that "there is not any thing, befalls any by chance, or *without* his providence," we must understand that the sense of "outside" is what is intended. Or, in the opening statement of chapter 9, we read that God has "indued" the will of man with certain things. What does this mean? It is important to know that it is a formal term with a very specific sense.

In order to work with all of these words properly, it is essential to have reliable dictionaries close at hand. But these reference works must be chosen very carefully, or the student may be easily misled.

Almost all words go through stages of development. Perhaps when they are first utilized, they have a quite specific referent. But as time passes, they may take on new senses, operate metaphorically, or even change completely. Take for example, the word "passion(s)." Historically, this word has generally though not universally been used with negative connotations.[1] Passions were sinful—they were not the equivalent of

---

[1] See Samuel Renihan, ed., *God Without Passions: A Reader* (Palmdale: RBAP, 2014), 40-42 for an example of a more positive use of "passions."

"emotions" generally, but rather described the worst parts of humanity's sinful expressions. Even today, most English translations of the Bible use "passion(s)" with an evil connotation. Our modern use of the term, however, is very different. To be "passionate" about something is often virtuous.[2] If we mistakenly import the familiar sense of this term into its use in the Confession, we run the risk of a serious misunderstanding of its doctrine. We need tools to give historical and theological perspective on key terms.

Vocabulary in General

Broadly speaking, there are two differing types of dictionaries. We may describe them as *synchronic* and *diachronic*. A synchronic dictionary primarily deals with words at a particular period in their development, most frequently contemporaneous with the publication date of the volume. Probably the majority of dictionaries for sale at the local bookstore are synchronic. They describe words as they have been recently and are being currently employed, normally omitting archaic terms and/or antiquated senses of recent

---

[2] We do, however, speak of "crimes of passion."

words. These types of dictionaries are very useful for most everyday needs,[3] but might not be for research into more ancient texts. In some cases, they may actually mislead the student.

A diachronic dictionary follows a different methodology. Its purpose is more historical, seeking to trace the usage of a word throughout its development. Recognizing that language is inherently fluent, subject to changes due to factors such as time and cultural differences,[4] the lexicographers involved in producing this type of reference work endeavor to demonstrate the stages, accretions, and alterations through which the words of the language have passed. For students of historical

---

[3] There are also historically-oriented synchronic dictionaries. See for example, David Crystal, *Shakespeare's Words: A Glossary and Language Companion* (London: Penguin Books, 2002); John Orchard Halliwell-Phillipps, *A Dictionary Of Archaic And Provincial Words: Obsolete Phrases, Proverbs And Ancient Customs From The Fourteenth Century* (Whitefish, MT: Kessinger Publications, 2006).

[4] When the Englishman, standing next to his automobile, speaks of the boot and the bonnet, the American may not realize that he refers to the trunk and the hood. And when the American asks his British friend for a lift, he is not requesting a ride on the elevator! We might remember Churchill's quip that England and America consist of "two peoples divided by a common language."

works, a dictionary of this type is indispensable. The assistance provided by such a reference work is enormous.

Without question, the *Oxford English Dictionary* (OED) is the finest diachronic work available in our language. It is definitive; a magisterial production in every way. For the student of English vocabulary, it is immensely useful.[5] Available in a variety of forms, everyone interested in 2LCF should obtain a copy and keep it close at hand.[6]

The best edition is the complete 20 volume set (with three supplemental volumes) currently in print. The drawback is that it will cost you upwards of $900.00, a price too rich for most of our book accounts. Of course, it should be accessible in a nearby library — if your local public library does not own the series, probably the nearest University or College will have it in the reference room of its collection. There will be times in your study of 2LCF that the effort to

---

[5] Bauer, Danker, Arndt & Gingrich, *A Greek-English Lexicon of the New Testament and Other Early Christian Literature* is a good example of a diachronic dictionary through a period of roughly 400 years.

[6] It really is valuable for any reading done on older English texts — Reformers, Puritans, Eighteenth-Century Evangelicals, etc.

obtain information from OED will be worth the trouble taken.

Alternatively, one might look for the older 12 volume edition in used bookstores. While not so up to date as the larger version, it is nevertheless exceedingly helpful for study of seventeenth-century documents. But even more easily reached by all of us is the two volume miniaturized edition. This is *not* an abridged or condensed version of OED. In this printing, the publishers took each page of the original text, reduced it in size by about 75%, and printed four of these smaller pages on one large page. The end result is that when the reader opens the book, the two pages facing him contain the image of 8 pages of the larger edition. Of course, almost none of us can read this tiny text; but the two volumes were issued in box sets with an accompanying magnifying glass. Generally, these sets can be found on the used market[7] for around $60.00, but I once purchased a set, in nice condition with the magnifying glass in the drawer at the top of the box, for $10.00 at the local equivalent of a Salvation Army Thrift Store. Bargains may be found in odd places.

---

[7] They seem to be always available on eBay.

The OED allows us to trace the history of the development of words in the English language. In each entry, it provides illustrations, which often are from the seventeenth century and, interestingly, frequently from religious books. Probably the largest segment of the book publishing industry in London in the seventeenth century was theology books, so the editors of OED make use of sermons, commentaries, and theology books to help us understand what words meant at the time. I've found this incredibly useful.

One might consider the meaning of the word "communion." I have argued that in the seventeenth century, the word "communion" served as the functional equivalent of the word we would use today for "to associate."[8] The OED is incredibly helpful in pinpointing the sense of that term. Whatever the form chosen, OED is in fact essential for the student of 2LCF. Careful and judicious use of its varied helps will provide wonderful insights and prevent misunder-standings and mistakes in interpretation.

---

[8] See chapter 6 of *Edification and Beauty*.

Theological Vocabulary in Particular

The vocabulary of the Confession when written was the common vocabulary of the literate English populace, comprehensible to any reader of the language. But it was also the technical vocabulary of divinity at a particular point of theological development—the end of the post-Reformation era. As such, it is deeply rooted in a long Christian tradition of carefully formulated doctrinal statements, precisely expressed and accepted across a wide range of "denominations" (to use the term anachronistically) as the specialized terminology of theological formulation. Any interpretation of the Confession (and of any other religious writing of the era) must be informed by a careful understanding of the technical nature of these terms.

We are deeply in debt to Richard Muller, who has produced what is, in my opinion, the single most useful work to assist our understanding of 2LCF, his *Dictionary of Latin and Greek Theological Terms*. While not written as an aid for any specific confessional interpretation, it is nevertheless directly relevant to all of the Reformation and post-Reformation era creedal statements. Organized alphabetically, it contains a host of entries germane to almost every chapter and paragraph. Though the terms themselves are in Latin or Greek, there is a helpful index of English terms, making the book useful for all students. Additionally, the text is thoroughly cross-referenced, so that the reader is able to follow threads of thought very easily.

An example of the usefulness of this dictionary is in order. Have you ever noticed that in the technical trinitarian language of chapter 2, paragraph 3, of 2LCF, the editors employed the term "subsistences" rather than the more common and recognizable "persons"? This change reflects a very careful and precise alteration, dependent on an acquaintance with centuries of detailed theological discussion. The change reflects sensitivity to a problem stemming from the limitations of human language—how can finite mortals express the ineffable? Muller's entries under *essentia, modus subsistendi, natura, persona, subsistentia, substantia* and *trinitas* are excellent summations of the history, development, and senses of the various technical terms. When I read them, and consider the beauty of the language of our Confession as it seeks to express the glories of God *in these terms*, I am inevitably brought to worship. One understands why our forefathers adopted this rendering, and the rich heritage that belongs to us through it. The contents of the book are theological gold. *Tolle Lege*.

The Words of the Confession

5.
The Puritan Confessional Context

It will help us to set some context by considering a couple of paragraphs from what was called the epistle *To the Judicious and Impartial Reader*. Hopefully, all of us will be judicious and impartial readers! One of the concerns I have about the Confession in the twentieth and twenty-first century is that it's often printed by itself without the epistle and without the appendix. It ought always to be printed with the epistle and with the appendix, because they really set the context for what's going on in the whole document. Here are some words from this epistle:

> One thing that greatly prevailed with us to undertake this work, was (not only to give a full account of our selves, to those

> Christians that differ from us about the subject of Baptism, but also) the profit that might from thence arise, unto those that have any account of our labors, in their instruction, and establishment in the great truths of the Gospel . . .

This was written in 1677, but that's basically what that famous statement about subscription we noted earlier says.

Carrying on:

> . . . in the clear understanding, and steady belief of which, our comfortable walking with God, and fruitfulness before him, in all our ways, is most nearly concerned; and therefore we did conclude it necessary to expresse our selves the more fully, and distinctly; and also to fix on such a method as might be most comprehensive of those things which we designed to explain our sense, and belief of; and finding no defect, in this regard, in that fixed on by the assembly . . .

In 1677, everybody who read this would have instantly known they were referring to the Westminster Assembly, so the "that fixed on by the assembly" is WCF.

> . . . and after them by those of the Congregational way . . .

That is shorthand for the Savoy Synod and its *Declaration*, so we find explicit reference to both the Westminster Assembly and the Savoy Synod of 1658. Because of what they had written,

> . . . we did readily conclude it best to retain the same order in our present confession: and also, when we observed that those last mentioned . . .

That is, "those of the Congregational way," the men of the Savoy Synod, which is John Owen, Thomas Goodwin, and others.

> . . . those last mentioned, did in their confession (for reasons which seemed of weight both to themselves and others) choose not only to express their mind in words concurrent with the former in sense . . .

If you look at Savoy, it very closely (and purposefully) resembles WCF.

> . . . concerning all those articles wherein they were agreed, but also for the most part

> without any variation of the terms we did in like manner conclude it best to follow their example in making use of the very same words with them both, in these articles (which are very many) wherein our faith and doctrine is the same with theirs, and this we did, the more abundantly, to manifest our consent with both, in all the fundamental articles of the Christian Religion, as also with many others, whose orthodox confessions have been published to the world; on behalf of the Protestants in divers Nations and Cities: and also to convince all, that we have no itch to clogge Religion with new words, but do readily acquiesce in that form of sound words, which hath been, in consent with the holy Scriptures, used by others before us . . .

They're saying when there is commonality between the three confessions of faith, there is complete agreement between those three documents. That sets a context for how we can understand what we find in our Confession of Faith. They're saying if you want to know what something in the Confession means and it's shared in common by the three documents, then go and read any of the authors who write about this who would have subscribed to any of those confessions of faith and you will be able to learn what they mean. You look at the broader context. You see what the Puritans say, what they're writing. They're explicitly stating their agreement.

Then notice the next terms they use.

> . . . hereby declaring before God, Angels, & Men . . .

That's similar to the language Paul uses three times in the Pastorals where he exhorts Timothy, "I charge you before God and the Lord Jesus Christ and the elect angels . . ." (1 Tim. 5:21, 6:13-14, 2 Tim. 4:1ff.). Our Fathers use that language; that's how serious they are.

> . . . hereby declaring before God, Angels, & Men, our hearty agreement with them, in that wholesome Protestant Doctrine, which with so clear evidence of Scriptures they have asserted: some things indeed, are in some places added, some terms omitted, and some few changed, but these alterations are of that nature, as that we need not doubt, any charge or suspition of unsoundness in the faith, from any of our brethren upon the account of them.
>
> In those things wherein we differ from others, we have exprest our selves with all candor and plainness that none might

> entertain jealousie of ought secretly lodged in our breasts . . .

This is one of the charges that had been made in the 1640s against the Particular Baptists when they first appeared in London. For example, Daniel Featley, a man who was briefly a member of the Westminster Assembly, wrote this about the First London Baptist Confession:

> if we give credit to this Confession and the Preface thereof, those who among us are branded with that title [i.e. Anabaptist], are neither Hereticks, nor Schismatics, but tender hearted Christians: upon whom, through false suggestions, the hand of authority fell heavy, whilst the Hierarchy stood: for, they neither teach free-will; nor falling away from grace with the *Arminians*, nor deny originall sinne with the *Pelagians*, nor disclaim Magistracy with the *Jesuites*, nor maintain plurality of Wives with the *Poloygamists*, nor community of goods with the *Apostolici*, nor going naked with the *Adamites*, much less aver the mortality of the soul with the *Epicures* and *Psychophannichists*: and to this purpose they have published this confession of Faith,

> subscribed by sixteen persons, in the name of seven Churches in *London*.[1]

But Dr. Featley didn't accept the integrity of the Baptists' language, for he then wrote:

> they cover a little rats-bane in a great quantity of sugar, that it may not be discerned: for, among the fifty three Articles of their Confession, there are not above sixe but may passe with a fair construction: and in those six, none of the foulest and most odious positions, wherewith that Sect is aspersed, are expressed.

Featley was incorrect, and this kind of scurrilous language ought to be condemned. Nevertheless, rumor and innuendo propagated by prominent opponents required the Baptists to claim and demonstrate their orthodoxy. In 2LCF, the Particular Baptists are once again making a point they had made 30 years before, saying, "This really is what we believe, and there's nothing hidden that we say or do behind closed doors." Back to the Epistle:

---

[1] Daniel Featley, *The Dippers Dip't or, The Anabaptists Duck'd and Plung'd over Head and Eares, at a Disputation in Southwark*, 6th ed. (London: Richard Cotes, 1651), 177-78.

> . . . In those things wherein we differ from others, we have exprest our selves with all candor and plainness that none might entertain jealousie of ought secretly lodged in our breasts, that we would not the world should be acquainted with; yet we hope we have also observed those rules of modesty, and humility, as will render our freedom in this respect inoffensive, even to those whose sentiments are different from ours.

One of the great things about the appendix is the way the Particular Baptists modestly express their views of believer's baptism. They don't provoke the paedobaptists with confrontational language. Rather they say, "We're convinced from Scripture of our doctrine of believer's baptism, and here's our explanation of it. Please receive it from us humbly." If you read that appendix, you really will be blessed by the tone in which they present themselves. It's very well done.

To drive this home, we should speak again about the family tree of our Confession of Faith just for a moment. The grandparent is WCF, which appears in 1646 and 1647. There is an interesting and seldom remembered story about the two versions of WCF—a story that's not often told. When first published, there were two slightly different editions. The one we most commonly see is not actually the one that was approved by Parliament. When the text was initially submitted by the Assembly to Parliament, Parliament required some edits. The members weren't satisfied with the version they received, what became the common version we usually see. We know it because it was taken to Edinburgh, printed there, and through the Scottish influence has become the standard version. Parliament edited and issued a slightly altered version of the Westminster Confession. That's probably the one our fathers used when they put together our Confession; the Parliamentary, rather than what we might call the Scottish version. Copies of the Parliamentary version are very difficult to find, even in the digital archives to which we might have access.

In addition to the WCF, there is the Savoy of 1658, which was the Congregationalists' revision of the Westminster Confession. If WCF is the grandparent of 2LCF, Savoy is the parent. The Savoy men purposely added to their Confession something they called the *Platform of Polity*, which was a lengthy statement of how they viewed the doctrine of the church to be practiced among the congregational churches.

They purposely separated out the *Platform of Polity* because they didn't want to make it equal to an article of faith. They viewed the Confession, the *Savoy Declaration* itself, as an article of faith that everyone ought to believe, but because the *Platform of Polity* was the area of difference between the Presbyterians and the Congregationalists, they segregated it out to say, "These are our views, but we won't treat them at the same high level that we'll treat the rest of the doctrines in the Confession of Faith itself."

When our Baptist fathers (probably Coxe and Collins) were editing 2LCF, they would have had the [Parliamentary?] *Westminster Confession* on the table. They would have had the *Savoy Declaration* and the *Platform of Polity*. They had a copy of the *First London Confession*, the 1646 version, on the table, and these were the primary documents behind our Confession of Faith. Of course, they would have had a Hebrew Old Testament, a Greek New Testament, and a King James Version Bible on the table with them as well.

Interestingly, our fathers took material from the *Platform of Polity* (which had been segregated out by the Congregationalists) and put much of it back into chapter 26. The

Baptists intentionally raised it to the level of an article of faith, but that makes sense. Our doctrine of the church is our distinctive practice. It's who we are as Particular Baptists, or, to use the modern term, Reformed Baptists. We are distinct from others because of our ecclesiology, and so our fathers saw fit to raise this up to the level of an article of faith. That's why chapter 26 is the longest chapter in our Confession of Faith.

6.
Important Helps

Let's think about some important helps. One of the most frequently asked questions I receive is something like this: "Are there any seventeenth-century Baptist expositions of the Confession?" I am not aware of any, but I do not know of any seventeenth-century expositions of the *Westminster Confession* or *Savoy Declaration* either. This does not, however, mean that we are without relevant primary source materials. There is something close: David Dickson's *Truth's Victory Over Error*.[1] The modern subtitle is not exactly accurate. It says, *A Commentary on the Westminster Confession of Faith*. While it

---

[1] David Dickson, *Truth's Victory over Error: A Commentary on the Westminster Confession of Faith* (Edinburgh: The Banner of Truth Trust, 2007 reprint).

technically isn't a commentary on WCF, it's as close as you can get to an interpretation of it in the seventeenth century. David Dickson (1583-1663) was a Scotsman, a contemporary seventeenth-century theologian and a well-known minister and professor of the Kirk. Several of his commentaries on books of the Bible have been reprinted in the last few decades.[2] A respected defender of the orthodox Reformed faith, Dickson used the WCF as the means of refuting a wide variety of heterodoxies, heresies, and theological mistakes. He worked his way through the Confession, dealing with various ancient and/or current differences of opinion, deviations, or false doctrines, showing how the Confession refuted those errors in his own century. In so doing, he has provided us with a contemporary exposition of large parts of that Confession—when 2LCF uses the same or similar language, we may assume that Dickson's comments help us. There is, however, a lot of material in the Confession that doesn't get treated at all in this book. That's why it's not really a commentary; it's Dickson's treatment of controversial issues and how they are refuted by the Confession of Faith.

---

[2] Psalms, Matthew, and Hebrews are all available.

Nevertheless, it is incredibly helpful and very, very useful. So far as we know, it's the only work of its kind from the seventeenth century on WCF.

A wonderful illustration is provided in his comments on WCF 21.3 (2LCF 22.3) which describes acceptable prayer in a variety of ways, ending with the phrases "if vocal, in a known tongue."[3] Several times, I have received communications asking if this statement somehow opened the door to a private prayer language, i.e., speaking in tongues! I have assured my correspondents that this was not the case, but they have wanted proof. When I read them the following words from Dickson, they were convinced and relieved:

> Quest. VI. *If Prayer be Vocal, ought it to be in a known tongue?*
>
> Yes. 1 *Cor.* 14. 14.
>
> Well then, *do not the* Papists *err*, who maintain, *that it is not needful, that publick prayers be in a known tongue; but that it is*

---

[3] 2LCF and Savoy read "when with others, in a known tongue." The difference in sense is minor and maintains the point made in the text above.

> *often-times expedient, that prayers be performed, in a tongue unknown to the Common-people?*
>
> Yes.
>
> *By what reasons are they confuted?*
>
> 1st, Because, the Apostle teaches expressly the contrary; 1 *Cor.* 14. 9,12. 2nd, Because, prayers celebrated in an unknown tongue, are not for edification, 1 *Cor.* 14. 14. 3rd, Because, he that occupieth the room of the unlearned (that is, who understands not strange tongues) cannot say Amen; 1 *Cor.* 14. 16. 4th, Because, the Lords prayer which is the special Rule of all our prayers, was prescribed in a tongue at that time best known.[4]

From this, it is evident that the object of the Confession's statement is the Romanist Latin mass, and in no way opens the door to the charismatic practice of tongues speaking. In my own study, I have found Dickson's contemporary explanation of much of WCF to be extremely helpful. It gives me a clear entry into the theological world of the era, and helps me to grasp the sense of the doctrine without

---

[4] Dickson, *Truth's Victory*, 113.

importing later, modern notions. I cannot recommend this tool highly enough.

While this is the only direct work on any of the relevant Confessions, it is not the only source of helpful information for our examination. We might say that many of the Reformation and/or Puritan era theological treatises may be of benefit for us (see bibliography below). But for the sake of space, we are highlighting the best of the best. Perhaps the most important person, we might even say a towering figure, for the theology of 2LCF, is John Owen. His 16 volume collected works, as well as his Hebrews commentary and the recently translated *Biblical Theology*, are a treasure chest of information and aid for the student.

Everyone ought to buy hard copies of all the published works of Owen. It is also helpful to supplement these with an electronic copy of the same works. This provides access to the contents of the writings. Though the indices of the Owen set are good, the indexing capabilities of modern software programs are superior. It is very simple to search for a particular phrase or term. When I have a question about these, this is one of my first and usually most helpful resources.

While there are no extant published seventeenth-century expositions of any of the three relevant Confessions, there are several commentaries on the *Westminster Shorter* and *Larger Catechisms*. Since the Westminster standards are considered to be of a piece, comments on the related areas of the Catechism may shed much helpful light on the doctrines of the Confessions. Of course, the student must be cautious and seek to ensure that he relates the proper question and answer to the chapter and paragraph in question—but this is usually fairly simple to do. The bibliography below points to several of these; students will recognize that those by John Flavel, Thomas Ridgely, Thomas Vincent, and Thomas Watson are contemporaneous with the era of 2LCF.

Slightly later, but nevertheless of great value, is the recently reprinted work of Benjamin Beddome, *A Scriptural Exposition of the Baptist Catechism*.[5] The *Baptist Catechism* was a minor revision of the *Westminster Shorter Catechism*,[6] published around 1693, and became

---

[5] Benjamin Beddome, *A Scriptural Exposition of the Baptist Catechism* (Birmingham, AL: Solid Ground Christian Books, 2006 reprint).

[6] Though there is some material taken from the *Westminster Larger Catechism* as well.

a source of instruction in Baptist homes for many years. Beddome, pastor of the Particular Baptist church in Bourton-on-the-Water in the Cotswolds of England, published his work in 1752. It is a wonderful summary of Christian doctrine, and provides us with an almost contemporary view of the doctrines contained in it. Beddome himself held to all of the doctrines of the Confession, and can be trusted as a guide to its teaching. His work is no less valuable for the student of 2LCF than those of Flavel, Ridgely, Vincent, and Watson.

One should also consider the proof texts. The WCF was first published without proof texts. When it was initially submitted to Parliament, it was sent back to the Assembly, requiring proof texts to be added. The reason they didn't initially have them was because the Assembly members believed that, in a sense, proof texts would distract from the fact that the Confession was a system that was taught in the entire Bible. For the Westminster divines, to tie the Confession to particular proof texts is to miss the point that its theology reflects all of Scripture, not simply a specific place in Scripture. Yet because of the demand of Parliament, they had to incorporate them. In 2LCF, our fathers included them as well. The proof texts point the reader to what may be called the *exegetical tradition*, that is, the long history of commentaries that were present and used by our fathers, accessible to them, and in which the doctrines of the Confession are established on the basis of the exegesis of Scripture. The proof texts are not specifically intended to be the only place where one would find that specific doctrine. In a sense, with the proof texts, the editors say, "Go back and read the commentaries and see how, in the commentaries, our exegetes ground the faith we believe, our doctrine, in the text of Scripture."

An example of certain of the commentaries they might have sometimes consulted (although there are many) is *Matthew Poole's Commentary*. Benjamin Keach frequently quotes from Poole. He doesn't even name Poole. He just says, "our annotators," and he means Poole when he does that.[7] Others might include John Trapp, who was a contemporary and did a five-

---

[7] Matthew Poole did not complete his English language exposition of Scripture, since he died when he came to about Isaiah 58. Others completed the process for him, so that when Keach relies upon Poole's commentary to support an argument, he refers to it as "our annotators" rather than by Poole's name.

volume commentary on the Old Testament which has been reprinted and is available today; the *Westminster Annotations*, which are hard to find, but were in a sense an attempt by the members of the Westminster Assembly to provide helps throughout the Bible; then, of course, individual commentaries on various books of the Bible: Henry Ainsworth on the Pentateuch[8] would be very important for the background of our Confession when it deals with the first five books of Moses; John Owen in his massive and magisterial commentary on the book of Hebrews[9] would be another example of a work to which they would send people to read.

---

[8] Henry Ainsworth, *Annotations on the Pentateuch, the Psalms of David and the Song of Solomon*, 2 vols. (Ligonier, PA: Soli Deo Gloria, 1991 reprint).

[9] Owen's work on Hebrews was partially released but still incomplete in 1677. The entire work was published by 1684.

7.
How the Confession is Organized

It is important to consider the internal structure of the Confession. The document may be considered in four main sections or units. Within each section, especially the second and third, the initial chapter of the unit gives the basic doctrine and the subsequent chapters then flesh out various aspects of that basic doctrine. In the sections, the first chapter of each gives the foundation that then is worked out in other places in the following chapters. Interestingly enough, almost every chapter is structured the same way, where the first paragraph of the chapter gives the basic doctrine, and the subsequent paragraphs of the chapter flesh out various aspects of that doctrine. There are one or two exceptions, but almost always that's the case. That structure helps us to think through what's going on in the section. It is as if the text says, "Here's the basic doctrine; and this is how it's worked out in various ways."

Additionally, it is imperative to note that 2LCF is a woven document. It must be read back and forth. What I mean by this is that, in the early part of the Confession of Faith, you have foundational doctrines that prepare the way for things that will be discussed in detail later. You need to always, at all times, ask yourself the question, when studying the earlier portions of the Confession, "What doctrine does this anticipate that may appear later on?" When you're later in the Confession, you must ask the question, "What does this fulfill? To what does this point backward? What's the basis, earlier on in the Confession, for this?" You must read it back and forth. Sometimes we approach the 32 chapters in 2LCF as if they are individual segments of doctrine that don't have a relationship to each other, when actually, it's very tightly woven together. You always must ask the question, "What does this anticipate?" or, "What does this fulfill?" back and forth, back and forth. Sometimes they'll be close together. Sometimes they'll be far apart. For example, the question of the immortality of the soul, which is addressed early on, is very important when we come to the doctrine of the resurrection at the end of the Confession. What it says in 31.1 about the immortality of the soul is based upon what we learn in chapter 4, "Of Creation." We must think back and forth all the time about the doctrines in the Confession. Another illustration might be to consider the doctrine of the Holy Spirit. There is no chapter devoted to the third Person of the Trinity (nor to the first Person either), but there is much teaching about the Holy Spirit knit into the fabric of the document. Like looking at a beautiful tapestry, we may notice the theme-strands about God's Spirit throughout.

Outline of the Confession[1]

At this point, let's think through the outline of the Confession. This is very important. I'm a big-picture person. I need to see the forest before I see the trees. I want to know the whole landscape. In order to understand the Confession and the development of doctrine in the Confession, the outline is very important. It breaks up into four parts: the first six chapters,

---

[1] See the Outline in alphanumeric format in the Appendix below.

which we may title, "First Principles." Then we have unit 2, "The Covenant." This is chapters 7–20 and followed by unit 3, "God-Centered Living: Freedom and Boundaries," chapters 21–30. Finally, "The World to Come," chapters 31 and 32. Let me go into more detail on this and explain to you what's happening in these four units.

Unit 1: First Principles (Chapters 1-6)

"First Principles" includes chapters 1–6. It commences with "Of the Holy Scriptures," the first chapter. In Reformed orthodox theology, this is called the *principium cognoscendi*, the principle of knowing. Muller's *Dictionary* defines it like this:

> [T]he *principium cognoscendi*, the principle of knowing or cognitive foundation, is a term applied to Scripture as the noetic or epistemological *principium theologiae*, without which there could be no true knowledge of God and therefore no theological system . . .[2]

---

[2] Muller, *Dictionary*, 288.

Why does our Confession of Faith begin with a chapter on the Scriptures? Because we can't know about subsequent confessional doctrines such as the trinitarian nature of God or his plan of salvation without the Scriptures. We must begin there. This is classic Reformed Scholastic theology, to begin with a chapter on the Scriptures, to set down the foundation, and give us the building blocks from which the rest of the doctrines are based. They're making a very important statement here that everything else that comes afterward is based upon, found in, and comes out of Scripture.

Then we move on to chapter 2. The second part of "First Principles" is the doctrine of God (which actually incorporates chapters 2-5). This is the *principium essendi*, the principle of being, which Muller defines this way:

> The *principium essendi*, the principle of being or essential foundation, is a term applied to God considered as the objective ground of theology without whom there could be neither divine revelation nor theology.[3]

We proceed from the principle of knowing to the principle of being, and we have God, so that

---

[3] Muller, *Dictionary*, 288.

we are presented with the reality of who God is. If we don't have this and if we don't get it down just right, then we can't move forward with our theology at all. Again, this is just classic Reformed Orthodox Scholastic theology in confessional form. In the seventeenth century, everyone would have recognized this immediately.

In the doctrine of God, then, we have chapter 2, "Of God and the Holy Trinity," which speaks to God's nature; chapter 3, "Of God's Decree," which speaks of the decrees of God. Let us pause for just a moment in order to understand the order of chapters and doctrines here. At this point in its exposition of doctrine, the *Baptist Catechism* asks the question, "What are the decrees of God?" It answers: "The decrees of God are his eternal purpose according to the counsel of his will, whereby, for his own glory, he hath foreordained whatsoever comes to pass." Then the next question is important: "How doth God execute his decrees?" The answer is, "God executeth his decrees in the works of creation and providence." Now back to the Confession. Think about the structure here. You have the principle of knowledge, the Holy Scriptures. You have the principle of being, which is the whole unit, and then you have God's nature, God's decree, and then, "How does God execute his decree?" In the works of creation and providence. The next chapter: "Of Creation," and then chapter 5, "Of Providence." You see, this is very familiar territory, but this is the way they thought about foundational doctrines. We have God's internal being, his work *ad intra*, and his work *ad extra* in creation and providence. Then, a necessary doctrine preparing to move forward is the chapter "Of the Fall of Man, of Sin, and of the Punishment Thereof." Those are the first principles. That's the foundation upon which we begin to build a system of theology.

Unit 2: The Covenant

God's work *ad extra* continues to be addressed in unit 2, which speaks of the plan, accomplishment and application of redemption by way of *covenant*. B. B. Warfield, in his work, *The Westminster Assembly and Its Work*, writes about "The architectonic principle" of the Westminster Confession. That's great language. It just means the skeleton, the architecture, the two-by-fours, four-by-sixes, or whatever they are that you build on.

> The architectonic principle of the Westminster Confession is supplied by the schematization of the Federal [covenant] theology, which had obtained by this time in Britain, as on the Continent, a dominant position as the most commodious mode of presenting the *corpus* of Reformed doctrine.[4]

To simplify, the skeleton of this part of the Confession is the doctrine of the covenant. That's very, very important to understand, because it provides the clue to the structure of chapters 7–20. Salvation is accomplished by means of covenant. Notice how this is very interestingly presented. In this case, 2LCF revises the WCF material to cast it more directly into a Baptist mold. Chapter 7 itself . . . (do you remember what was said above? The first chapter at the head of the unit provides the basic doctrine) Chapter 7, "Of God's Covenant," describes to us, from a Baptist perspective, the nature of covenant theology. We have God's covenant defined for us in chapter 7, then we have "Of Christ the Mediator," the covenant head, presented to us.

---

[4] B. B. Warfield, *The Westminster Assembly and its Work* (Grand Rapids: Baker Books, 1981 reprint), 56. We must remember that 2LCF follows the structure of WCF, thus the quotation applies to both Confessions.

If you look at the end of chapter 7 and the beginning of chapter 8, they're intimately tied together by reference to the covenant of redemption. You can't miss it. Chapter 8 is placed where it is purposely to speak about Christ as the head of the covenant. He's the one who brings it to pass.

Then chapter 9, "Of Free Will," presents to us the covenantal setting, which is what the covenant is about: God's purpose of salvation. This unit focuses on the covenant of grace. It moves forward to speak to us about salvation, and as a result we need to think about man's will as he is created, then as he is fallen and in need of covenantal grace, renewed as exercised in covenantal grace, and then perfected. These three chapters (7-9) prepare the way for a discussion of salvation. The first, chapter 7, lays down the basis. Chapter 8 shows us Christ. Chapter 9 provides us with some information about the states of humanity, helping us to move forward into the doctrine of salvation.

Have you ever noticed that the order of chapters 10–18 in our Confession does not follow our typical *ordo salutis*?[5] The most

---

[5] *Ordo salutis* is a Latin phrase which we might translate "order of salvation." Theologians use it to describe the theological order in which God gives the

obvious way to demonstrate this is to notice that chapter 11, "Of Justification," precedes chapter 14, "Of Saving Faith." Usually, when we talk about the *ordo salutis*, we speak about faith, which is the instrument of justification. Why did the confessors place justification before faith? That's an interesting question, and there's a very specific reason for the way chapters 10–18 of the Confession are ordered. This subsection addresses the blessings of salvation in two very specific subcategories. Chapters 10–13 and chapters 14-18. Chapters 10-13 are what might be called covenant blessings. That is, they describe the acts of God on behalf of his people to save them. Richard Muller, in his *Dictionary*, under the heading *foedus monopleuron*, says this about the covenant of grace:

> *one-sided or unilateral, covenant*; the covenant as bestowed by God and exhibiting his will toward humanity. Since the foundation of all divine covenants is the eternal will of God and the purpose of all divine covenants is ultimately the fulfillment of God's will to

---

blessings of salvation to us. For example, a typical *ordo salutis* list might be effectual calling, regeneration, faith and repentance, justification, adoption, sanctification, perseverance, assurance, glorification.

the glory of God alone, God's covenants—both the *foedus operum* [covenant of works] and the *foedus gratiae* [covenant of grace]—are declarations of the divine will towards man and thus one-sided, *monopleuron*, rather than being covenants arranged by the mutual consent of parties for their mutual benefit. Even though the covenants include human beings and are to their benefit, they have no part in the arrangement of the terms of the covenants, both of which are bestowed, as it were, from above.[6]

That's viewing the covenant of grace from the divine perspective and arguing that it is a one-sided covenant. So, what we have in the structure of the Confession here are first the acts of God in saving his people: Chapter 10, "Of Effectual Calling"—who does that? God the Holy Spirit does that, does he not? Chapter 11, "Of Justification"—who justifies us? It is God who justifies us, by Christ. Chapter 12, "Of Adoption"—who adopts us into his family? It is God who adopts us. Then chapter 13 is "Of Sanctification." Initially, the chapter describes God's work of setting us apart for himself, so we have presented to us the covenant blessings that come to us in salvation from the divine

---

[6] Muller, *Dictionary*, 129.

perspective, specifically what God does. The blessings of salvation always begin with God.

Yet then, in the next subcategory, we have what we might call covenant graces, which are the acts of man. Again, from Muller at the entry *foedus dipleuron*; (the previous term *monopleuron* means one-sided. *Dipleuron* means two-sided.)

> *two-sided or bilateral, covenant*; at the point at which a human being enters into God's covenant, receives the terms established by God, and, in effect becomes a partner in the covenant with God, the *foedus operum* and *foedus gratiae* can be termed bilateral covenants. . . . Since the covenant is ordained by God alone and cannot be entered by fallen humanity unless God provides the grace necessary to regenerate the will and draw man into covenant, the covenant is initially unilateral; but once an individual is drawn into the covenant and the will is regenerated, . . . the covenant appears as bilateral.[7]

Now the same covenant is considered from the human perspective. After God has acted, what do we do? Think about the order of the chapters here, for it is fascinating material.

---

[7] Muller, *Dictionary*, 127.

Covenant graces or man's acts: Chapter 14, "Of Saving Faith." Who believes? We do. Of course, saving faith must be granted to us; we don't become Pelagians at this point. God grants the faith, but we are the ones who believe. Chapter 15, "Of Repentance unto Life and Salvation," is the twin grace of faith. Who repents? We repent. Chapter 16, "Of Good Works." Who does the good works? Well, it's God's Holy Spirit working in us, but we do them. Chapter 17, "Of the Perseverance of the Saints." Notice it's not the *preservation* of the saints; it's the *perseverance* of the saints. We are preserved by grace, but here, based on the two-sided covenant, we are called to persevere. Chapter 18, "Of the Assurance of Grace and Salvation." God grants to us assurance, but who enjoys it? We do.

In chapters 14–18, we have the covenant viewed from a human perspective. It's now a *foedus dipleuron*. That's the structure of these chapters on the covenant. From this perspective, it makes sense why justification precedes saving faith, since it's God's act, and it must come first. These chapters could be ordered differently, according to the *ordo salutis* as we know it today, but that's the reason you have these chapters laid out the way they are. In this case, it protects the sovereignty of God.

Then there's one more subsection in the unit on the covenant (chapters 7-20), which is the means of receiving the covenant: chapter 19, "Of the Law of God," and chapter 20, "Of the Gospel and the Extent of Grace thereof." We are condemned and shown our sin by the law, and then the grace of God in the gospel and how it spreads around the world is stated to us. That's the second major section in the Confession: "Of God's Covenant."

Unit 3: God-centered Living — Freedom and Boundaries

Let's move onto unit 3. This is a really interesting section. The "First Principles" are in chapters 1-6. "The Covenant" is in 7-20. Then the third unit, "God-centered Living: Freedom and Boundaries." It may be that we don't understand and appreciate how important the doctrine of Christian liberty is. Three amazing quotations make this point. The first is from John Calvin, from Book III of the *Institutes*:

> We must now discuss Christian freedom. He who proposes to summarize gospel teaching ought by no means to omit an explanation

of this topic. For it is a thing of prime necessity, and apart from a knowledge of it consciences dare undertake almost nothing without doubting; they hesitate and recoil from many things; they constantly waver and are afraid. But freedom is especially an appendage of justification and is of no little avail in understanding its power. Indeed, those who seriously fear God will enjoy the incomparable benefit of this doctrine . . . But, as we have said, unless this freedom be comprehended, neither Christ, nor gospel truth, nor inner peace of soul, can be rightly known.[8]

Christian liberty is intimately tied to the doctrine of justification. A Christian can hardly act without a proper understanding of it. Does John Calvin think the doctrine is important?

The second is from that great Puritan John Owen:

The second principle of the Reformation, whereon the reformers justified their separation from the church of Rome, was this: "That Christian people were not tied up unto blind obedience unto church-guides,

---

[8] John Calvin, *Institutes of the Christian Religion*, ed. John T. McNeill (Philadelphia: The Westminster Press, 1960 translation), III.xix.1(1:833-34).

but were not only at liberty, but also obliged to judge for themselves as unto all things that they were to believe and practice in religion and the worship of God." They knew that the whole fabric of the Papacy did stand on this basis or dunghill, that the mystery of iniquity was cemented by this device,—namely, that *the people were ignorant*, and to be kept in ignorance, being obliged in all things unto an implicit obedience unto their pretended guides.[9]

"The second principle of the Reformation . . ." John Owen makes this point very clearly. Christian liberty is at the very heart of the Reformation.

Our third witness is another English Puritan, Samuel Bolton, from his well-known book *The True Bounds of Christian Freedom*:

> There are two great things Christ has intrusted into the hands of his church: First, *Christian faith*. Secondly, *Christian liberty*: and as we are to contend earnestly for the maintenance of the faith, as the Apostle saith, Jude 3. So also for the maintenance of Christian *libertie*, against all oppugners and

---

[9] John Owen, *Works* (Edinburgh: The Banner of Truth Trust, 1965 reprint), 15:402.

underminers of it, *Gal. 5.1. Stand fast in the liberty wherewith Christ has made you free.*[10]

That's from page 8 of the seventeenth-century version. In the Banner of Truth edition, it's on page 20. It's slightly modernized, but it's basically the same thing. This is pretty powerful, isn't it?

This is what our Puritan fathers did: Chapter 20 in the WCF, or chapter 21 in the 2LCF (WCF doesn't have the chapter on the gospel, chapter 20, so the chapter numbers differ from this point onward) was not just placed in this position because something needed to be said about Christian liberty. Rather, this chapter was positioned at the head of an entire section, because it is of fundamental importance to understand. As a result, we have an entire unit, "God-Centered Living: Freedom and Boundaries," in which Christian liberty is worked out in many different ways. The basis of the doctrine is found in the first chapter (21), and it contains that great statement, "God alone is Lord of the conscience, and hath left it free from the doctrines and commandments of men

---

[10] Samuel Bolton, *The True Bounds of Christian Freedome* (London: Printed for P.S. 1656), 8.

. . ." That's the basis. Christ has purchased it for us. It belongs to us.

Yet how is it worked out? It's worked out in the following chapters. The principles of Christian liberty are given to us. The worship of God, in chapters 22 and 23. The regulative principle of worship was constructed to protect the liberty of God's people. Our fathers believed that anything that was introduced in worship which was not commanded in Scripture was an intrusion on the liberty of God's people. To make you do something in worship that God has not commanded is a violation of your liberty. That's why chapter 22 follows chapter 21. We have instruction in the practice of worship (so that our liberty is not violated), and then the day of worship, how we are to keep that day. That's a matter related to our liberty, isn't it? What obligation do I owe to the Lord on that day? What am I free to do or not to do? The doctrine of Christian liberty has a direct relationship to it.

Chapter 23, "Of Lawful Oaths and Vows," is an overlooked chapter. Chapter 23 begins with the words, "A lawful oath is a part of religious worship . . ." It's not about public worship, but private worship. Where am I bound and where am I free, in terms of oaths?

There were very practical applications of this in the seventeenth century, as there are also today.

Chapter 24, "Of the Civil Magistrate," addresses questions such as: What are our responsibilities to the duly constituted government in the place in which we live? Are we free to do as we please? It answers, no, there are restrictions to our liberty, and so that's defined for us. Chapter 25, "Of Marriage," speaks to important matters: Are we free to marry anyone? Are there any restrictions on our marriage? Chapter 25 addresses those questions. It gives us a definition that helps us to understand our Christian liberty in terms of marriage.

Then chapters 26–30, on the church, are another subsection. How do they relate to Christian liberty? Notice, sometime, when you read chapters 26–30, how frequently the lordship of Christ is emphasized there. Christian liberty is about obedience to Christ the Lord. The way our doctrine of the church is worked out is really an expression of what our Christian liberty is about. So, you have chapter 26, "Of the Church," which deals with the church universal and the church local. Chapter 27, "Of the Communion of Saints," is a neglected chapter, but a very important one that talks about our obligations to others. When someone is in need, what do I need to do to help? What are my obligations at that moment?

Chapter 28 is "Of Baptism and the Lord's Supper." It gives the basic doctrine. Observe how the first paragraph, at least four times, emphasizes the fact that Christ is the Lord over baptism. They almost overdo it, perhaps in imitation of the apostle Paul. He just keeps going with something. It's as if he wants to say, "Are you getting my point?" That's what they're saying to us. "Are you getting the point? We practice what we practice because Christ is Lord over baptism and we must obey him, not the traditions that come to us from Rome. We must obey him and give baptism only to those who are able to profess their faith." Chapter 29 works that out in more detail, and then, of course, chapter 30, "Of the Lord's Supper." That's the third section of the Confession, and it all relates to questions of Christian liberty.

Unit 4: The World to Come

Finally, we have the fourth section of the Confession. We have "First Principles," "The Covenant," "God-Centered Living: Freedom and Boundaries," and "The World to Come." There we have chapters 31 and 32, "Of the State of Man after Death, and of the Resurrection of the Dead," the intermediate and resurrection states, and then, finally, chapter 32, "Of the Last Judgement." That's how it's put together. That's certainly important material to assist us to think through the whole system. Why is it ordered the way it is? What were they thinking when they put it together? What were the reasons these chapters are placed where they are? It all makes sense when you see it put together in that way: the "First Principles," the well-known, well-established Reformed Scholastic principles of knowing and being, the doctrine of God. Then "The Covenant," moving toward God's blessings in salvation, "Christian Liberty," the "second principle of the Reformation," and then, finally, of course, "The World to Come."

8.
The Doctrinal Emphases of the Confession

A survey of 2LCF suggests that it has certain doctrinal emphases which are similar though not identical to the outline just given. They are significant and must be mentioned. They provide some of the distinctive emphases of the Confession.

Catholic

First, we must emphasize that the Confession is a catholic document. We should not be troubled by this term, in fact it needs to be reclaimed from its misuse by the Roman Catholic denomination. We are catholic Christians; by this we mean to say that we are committed to all the doctrines believed by Christians throughout the history of the church of Jesus Christ. Catholic simply means *universal*, and this concept is very important. Because of our human limitations, we tend to think horizontally about the church as it is *now* on earth. But we must think vertically, for the church consists of all God's elect from all time. Enoch, Noah, Abraham and Sarah, Jacob, Ruth, David, Isaiah, John the Baptist, Paul, Timothy, Irenaeus, Athanasius, Augustine, Bradwardine, Luther, Calvin, Kiffin, Gill, Spurgeon, etc. All are saved by Jesus Christ and all these are brothers and sisters in the Lord. Writing in the fifth century, Vincent of Lerins, commenting on 1 Timothy 6:20[1] stated:

> "Keep the deposit." What is "The deposit"? That which has been intrusted to thee, not that which thou hast thyself devised: a matter not of wit, but of learning; not of private adoption, but of public tradition; a matter brought to thee, not put forth by thee, wherein thou art bound to be not an author but a keeper, not a teacher but a disciple, not a leader but a follower.[2]

---

[1] "O Timothy, keep the deposit entrusted to you" (1 Tim. 6:20).

[2] Vincent of Lérins, *The Commonitory*, in *Nicene and Post-Nicene Fathers*, Second Series, vol. 11, eds. Phillip

Two examples will suffice: we see the presence of received catholic doctrine in the trinitarian language of chapter 2 and in the Chalcedonian language about the person of our Lord Jesus Christ in chapter 8. This is very important. Our Confession commits us to catholic orthodoxy.

Gospel-centered

In the second place, 2LCF is gospel-centered, and in two specific ways. It asserts that forgiveness of sin and the gift of eternal life comes only through faith in the Person and work of Jesus Christ. Salvation (as it is often called) comes solely and exclusively by faith alone through grace alone in Christ alone. Our works, ethnicity, religious acts, etc. are all null and void; we find justification only through dependence on Christ. He was promised in the words spoken to the serpent in the garden, a pledge expanded throughout the Old Testament, he is truly God and truly man, two natures united forever in one person, he lived a life of perfect holy obedience to the law of God, died at Calvary to satisfy the demands of divine justice, rose bodily from the dead, ascended

---

Schaff and Henry Wace, trans. C. A. Heurtley, vol. 11 (1894; reprint, Peabody: Hendrickson, 2004), 147.

into heaven and will return to establish his eternal kingdom.

On the other hand, 2LCF asserts that the life of the believer, especially with reference to our duties and obligations, is always based in this gospel. The famous pattern of the *Heidelberg Catechism* (which is really the Reformed understanding of sanctification) Guilt/Grace/Gratitude is the pattern for living the Christian life. We were sinners, saved by grace, and in thankfulness we present our bodies as living sacrifices.

Covenantal

Thirdly, the Confession is covenantal. In the twentieth century, a novel, recent system of interpreting the Bible known as Dispensationalism overwhelmed the American evangelical churches. It teaches (in its older yet still popular version), among other things, that there must be a hard distinction maintained between Israel and the church, so that God's purpose is accomplished in two peoples of God. By implication, the Old Testament is for Israel and the New Testament for the church. The result is that many do not give proper emphasis to *all* of Scripture, viewing the Old Testament as less useful to Christians. But covenantalism is the ancient faith of Christians. It recognizes that the Bible itself is structured by covenants: in Genesis 3:15 we find the promise of the covenant of grace, and this promise is progressively revealed in the covenants with Noah, Abraham, Moses, and David until it comes to fruition in the new covenant ratified by the blood of Jesus. For this reason, it teaches us that salvation comes to humans by way of covenant. Our argument about the structure of 2LCF above demonstrates how this works.

Reformed, Calvinistic, Predestinarian

Fourthly, the doctrine the Confession teaches is Reformed, or some might say Calvinistic, or even Predestinarian in that it instructs us that God sovereignly saves sinners. The Synod of Dort published a series of Canons in 1618-19, addressing five objections to the Reformed doctrine of salvation which had been presented by a group called the Remonstrants. These Canons have often been summarized by the acronym TULIP: Total Depravity, Unconditional Election, Limited Atonement, Irresistible Grace, and Perseverance of the

Saints. Without using this language, 2LCF clearly teaches each of these doctrines.

Puritan

Fifth, we may say that it is a Puritan document. Puritanism is simply the English version of the Reformed faith and practice of the churches on the European continent. 2LCF expresses all of these common emphases—*Sola Scriptura, Sola Gratia, Sola Fidei, Solus Christus, Soli Deo Gloria.*

Baptist, Congregational, Independent

All the previous emphases share a common place with the broader Reformed (and often Lutheran) movement around them. The final emphasis to note is the most distinctive, in that 2LCF is a Baptist and Congregational or Independent[3] document, though even here it shares a common heritage. It is Congregational in that, like the *Savoy Declaration,* it denies any higher authority over the local church. Churches are autonomous, self-governing, and

---

[3] These two terms, "Congregational" and "Independent" were used interchangeably in the seventeenth century. Probably "Congregational" was the more common of the two.

have all power necessary within themselves to accomplish the task of discipline given to them by Christ, but at the same time they are not to be isolated. The doctrine of the church in the Confession is associational, recognizing that independent churches may and ought to join together to accomplish common causes.[4] It is also specifically Baptist in that it teaches that baptism is only for believers who profess their faith in Christ.

Conclusion

This summary helps us to understand that subscribing a Confession means much more than simply adopting a few tenets. Rather, it is to confess the whole counsel of God as it is summarized in the document. While TULIP may be one of the flowers in the garden, there are many more which capture our attention and admiration.

---

[4] See my *Associational Churchmanship: Second London Confession of Faith 26.12-15* (Palmdale, CA: RBAP, 2016).

9.
Editorial Principles

What about editorial principles? What about some of the changes that were made in the Confession? Our Confession of Faith largely follows the *Savoy Declaration*. In the book, *True Confessions*, one may see how the Savoy Puritans adopted and yet at points significantly changed the material from WCF, and our fathers followed their method. Most of the time when there are changes made, our fathers were following the Savoy. Sometimes, though, at least eleven times, they go back to the WCF and restore some of its readings. For example, in chapter 10, paragraph 3, the Baptists reintroduced the WCF phrase, ". . . through the Spirit . . ." We may know that on the editing table there was a copy of the WCF for consulting, and 11 times, they brought that material back into the Confession.

Some changes are expansions of thought. In chapter 11, "Of Justification," the Savoy saw the necessity of adding a statement about the imputation of Christ's active obedience to believers to the statement about the righteousness of Christ. This specific doctrine is not present in WCF. It's an interesting discussion as to why it's not present in Westminster, but beyond the scope of this book. Yet our Confession of Faith accepts this expansion and quite explicitly requires of us a doctrine of justification that includes the imputation of the righteousness of Christ.

Many changes are simply clarifications. For example, in Savoy and WCF, chapter 8, "Of Christ the Mediator," you'll notice that when they speak of our Savior's birth, they simply say he was of Mary's substance, but in the 2LCF, you have a much longer statement added. The reason for this is that among some of the General Baptists, i.e. the Arminian Baptists, there was an heretical Christology that denied the true humanity of Christ. In response and defense of orthodoxy, our fathers expanded on that statement, ". . . of her substance . . ." in some ways to go beyond the simple statement in order to make clear that the

Savior really and truly was a man like us. That's the reason for that clarification.

Another thing that's really, really important is that deletion of terms or phrases does not necessarily imply the rejection of a concept. That's a simple mistake some readers make. They say, "Oh look, it's not there. They must have rejected it." Well, if that's the case, sometimes the result is problematic. For example, notice in chapter 8, speaking about Christ's death: ". . . in his soul, and most painful sufferings in his body; was crucified, and died . . ." Then they left out the WCF and Savoy phrase, ". . . was buried . . ." Why isn't it there? Do you think they denied that he was buried? Obviously not. Sometimes, we need to remember that the Baptist Catechism helps us by working out the doctrines. Notice here in the Baptist Catechism:

> Q. 31. Wherein did Christ's humiliation consist?
>
> A. Christ's humiliation consisted in His being born, and that in a low condition, made under the law, undergoing the miseries of this life, the wrath of God, and the cursed death of the cross, in being buried, and continuing under the power of death for a time.

The Baptist Catechism is, in some ways, an expansion of thought of the 2LCF. They didn't deny at all that he was buried, so you should be really careful not to draw the wrong conclusion. Some say, "Look, the covenant of works is absent, so they denied it!" No. I wish I had time to refute that one. It's just not true.[1]

Additions are often expressions of specifically Baptist thought. In chapter 7, "Of God's Covenant," you'll notice the three Confessions are all different. Each one expresses the nuances of Presbyterian, Congregational, or Baptist covenantalism. They were not identical.

It is also helpful to realize there are printer's errors in both original and modern versions. Here is a most obvious instance. The first proof text listed at chapter 8.6 is "1 Corinthians 4:10." If one consults this text, it seems completely unrelated to the point made in 8.6. And that is a correct observation, for the correct text should be "1 Corinthians 10:4." As soon as 1 Corinthians 10:4 is consulted, it becomes apparent that the original is a mistake. Whoever was the printer who set the text

---

[1] For a thorough refutation of this notion see Richard C. Barcellos, *The Covenant of Works: Its Confessional and Scriptural Basis* (Palmdale, CA: RBAP, 2016).

reversed the 10 and the 4, and that error has been perpetuated in the modern editions. If you have a modern edition, you probably have that error in it.

Capitalization is generally unimportant. Punctuation is according to the archaic standards of the day in which it was first issued. At times a period is used at the end of a sentence, in others a colon serves the same purpose. The semicolons in the chapters of the Confession generally serve as dividing points. It is helpful to notice the beginning and the end of sections bounded by the semicolons. In most cases, they indicate that the phrases between them are a unit, so pay attention to those things. Don't just look at a word, but look at its context and notice the semicolons and how they mark out units of thought within the sentences.

As any other ancient document, 2LCF requires careful study. And since it claims to summarize the teaching of Scripture, expressing the things that must surely be believed, it deserves diligent, prayerful thought.

The concluding prayer of *To the Judicious and Impartial Reader* addresses this very well:

We shall conclude with our earnest prayer that the God of all grace will pour out those measures of his Holy Spirit upon us, that the profession of truth may be accompanied with the sound belief and diligent practice of it by us, that his name may in all things be glorified through Jesus Christ our Lord. Amen.

Editorial Principles

10.
The Baptist Catechism[1]

The Baptist Catechism is an extremely valuable supplement to 2LCF and should be regularly consulted as something of a cross-reference of theology. The Westminster Assembly recognized the potential benefits of the ancient method of teaching and simplifying theology by memorizing question and answer, and the Baptists followed suit. B. B. Warfield tells us that one of the authors of the *Westminster Shorter Catechism* (the document on

---

[1] Some of this material is taken from my introductions to the *Baptist Catechism* published in *The Baptist Confession of Faith & The Baptist Catechism* (Birmingham, AL and Carlisle, PA: Solid Ground Christian Books and Reformed Baptist Publications, 2010) and also to the pamphlet edition published by Reformed Baptist Publications.

which our Catechism is based) said that "they sought to set down in it not the knowledge the child has, but the knowledge the child ought to have."[2] The Assembly produced two catechisms. The *Larger Catechism* is a detailed learning device for theology; but more famous is the *Shorter Catechism* they published. The Puritan pastor Thomas Vincent said, "I know no catechism more full of light and sound doctrine,"[3] and he was not alone in his evaluation. Our Baptist fathers recognized the profound benefit found in its careful expressions, and knew that it could be of great benefit in their own churches.

Purpose

The Catechism was published under the title *A Brief Instruction in the Principles of Christian Religion: Agreeable to the Confession of Faith, put forth by the ELDERS and BRETHREN of many Congregations of Christians, (baptized upon*

---

[2] B. B. Warfield, *Is the Shorter Catechism Worth While?*, in *The Selected Shorter Writings of Benjamin B. Warfield*, vol. 1 (Nutley, NJ: Presbyterian and Reformed, 1970), 381.

[3] Thomas Vincent, *An Explicatory Catechism: or, An Explanation of the Assemblies Shorter Catechism* (Glasgow: Robert Sanders, 1674), sig A3 verso. The statement is reprinted in the Banner of Truth Paperback edition, viii.

Profession of their Faith) in London and the Country; owning the Doctrine of Personal Election, and Final Perseverance. The earliest known copy in existence states on the title page that it is the fifth edition, published in 1695. Since the request for its writing came in 1693, one presumes that the first four editions were printed between those dates; by 1703 it was in its tenth edition. This almost certainly refers to the number of times it was printed.

At the end of the text of the catechism, there is a note which reads:

> An Advertisement to the reader.
>
> Having a desire to shew our near Agreement with many other Christians, of whom we have great Esteem; we some Years since put forth a Confession of our Faith, almost in all Points the same with that of the *Assembly*, and *Savoy*, which was subscribed by the Elders and Messengers of many Churches baptized on profession of their Faith; and do now put forth a short Account of *Christian Principles*, for the Instruction of our Families, in most things agreeing with the *Shorter Catechism* of the *Assembly*. And this we were the rather induced to, because we have commonly made use of that *Catechism* in our Families:

And the Difference being not much, it will be more easily committed to Memory.[4]

Based on this information, we may say that there were at least two purposes in publishing this Catechism—to serve as an addendum and aid in understanding the Confession, and to provide a means by which families may learn its doctrines. The two documents were intended to supplement one another. The truths taught in the Confession were re-phrased in the Catechism. By learning it, one will have a good understanding of the doctrine of the Confession. In addition, an issue that may be obscure in one may be clarified in the other. Additionally, it was viewed as part of a long-term project in each Christian home, in which parents seek to develop a solid and sound understanding of the most basic truths of our faith.

Origin

At the 1689 General Assembly, William Collins, pastor of London's Petty France Church, was

---

[4] *A Brief Instruction in the Principles of Christian Religion* (London: Printed in the Year 1695), unnumbered verso of page 23.

asked to provide a Baptist version of the Assembly's Catechism. The minuted record states "That a Catechism be drawn up, containing the substance of the Christian religion, for the instruction of children and servants, and that brother William Collins be desired to draw it up."[5] Though frequently identified with Benjamin Keach, it is more likely to have been edited first by William Collins of London's Petty France church. Certainly, he was specifically requested to do this work, and there is no documentary evidence to assume otherwise. If in fact he had been co-editor of the Confession, it would make sense to ask him to edit the Catechism as well. The attribution of the Catechism to Benjamin Keach perhaps arises from later versions, possibly supplemented by him.

Structure

The Catechism is wonderfully organized. After some initial introductory questions about God and the Bible, question 7 asks, "What do the Scriptures principally teach?" and the answer is twofold: They teach us what we are to believe about God, which serves as the basis for

---

[5] Renihan, *Faith and Life for Baptists*, 134.

questions 8-44; and they teach us the duty that God requires of man, the basis for questions 45-87. This is followed by an explanation of our inability to keep these commands, and the necessity to believe the gospel and use the means of grace in questions 88-115. By the end, the student will have been exposed to a marvelous summary of the whole of Christian doctrine.

The reader will notice that the most significant changes to the *Shorter Catechism* were made in its first few questions. It seems that the Baptists sought to make the Catechism more personal by asking introductory questions about God and the Scriptures and humanity's obligations to him as he has revealed himself.

Not only is this Catechism an excellent summary of the Christian faith, it is also at times deeply moving in its expressions. As the learner proceeds through the series of questions and grasps the profound glory of the triune God, he will be moved to bow down and worship. When he memorizes the questions about the law, he will be burdened with his own sinfulness, and when he works his way through the questions and answers on the gospel, his heart will be full of love and thanksgiving to this great covenant-keeping

God. This is theology that moves the deepest recesses of the human soul—it challenges the intellect and feeds the heart with an abundance of profoundly stirring truth. It is exactly what every child—and may we say every adult—needs to help live a life to God's glory.

Helps

There are many valuable expositions of the Westminster *Shorter Catechism*. Three from the Puritan era are the previously mentioned exposition by Thomas Vincent, Thomas Watson's *Body of Divinity*,[6] and John Flavel's *An Exposition of the Assemblies Catechism*.[7] Each has

---

[6] Thomas Watson, *A Body of Practical Divinity, consisting of One Hundred Seventy Six Sermons on the Lesser Catechism* (London: Thomas Parkhurst, 1692). In the twentieth century it was reprinted in three volumes by the Banner of Truth under the titles *A Body of Divinity*, *The Ten Commandments,* and *The Lord's Prayer* (Edinburgh: The Banner of Truth Trust, 1983) and more recently by Solid Ground Christian Books under the title *A Complete Body of Divinity* (Birmingham, AL: Solid Ground Christian Books, 2016).

[7] John Flavel, *An Exposition of the Assemblies Catechism, with Practical Inferences from each Question* (London: Thomas Cockwell, 1692). This work is included in the Banner of Truth reprint of Flavel's *Works* (Edinburgh: The Banner of Truth Trust, 1982), 6:138-317.

proven to be useful to Christians and all are worth consulting. One advantageous factor in consulting these books is that they are careful expositions written by contemporaries, and based on sermons delivered to their congregations. Readers are helped to understand both the important doctrinal system of the *Catechism*, as well as the practical applications made by skillful preachers of God's Word.

Since we are considering the *Baptist Catechism*, we should emphasize that there is also an excellent and useful exposition of the *Baptist Catechism* (previously mentioned) done by Benjamin Beddome, pastor of the church in Bourton-on-the-Water in Gloucestershire, England, from 1740-95. His fruitful ministry profoundly affected many, and along with his many hymns, his exposition of the Catechism is of great benefit. Beddome's *Exposition* is especially useful in that it is full of Scripture and assists the student to understand how the doctrines of the Catechism are thoroughly grounded in the Word of God. Many have found Beddome's work to be useful and of much edification for study classes. By using these four easily accessible expositions, anyone will gain a first-rate understanding of the most important doctrines of the Christian faith.

11.
Conclusion: John Owen on Confessionalism

In conclusion we may ask, why are Confessions important? The great Puritan John Owen expresses beautifully the essence of confessionalism, and as confessional Reformed Baptists, his comments summarize our own convictions. Our doctrine of subscription evidences our genuine, truthful convictions, while at the same time expresses our allegiance to the best theological thinking of the catholic church of Jesus Christ. Protestant Confessions are not novelties. Their doctrines have deep roots extending all the way back to the Church Fathers. This is from Owen's brief 1667 tract *A Peace-Offering* (1667).

For the faith which we profess, and which we desire to walk according unto, we need not insist upon the particular heads of it, having some years since, in our confessions, publicly declared it, with the joint consent of all our churches, neither do we own or avow any doctrine but what is therein asserted and declared. And we hope it will not be looked upon as an unreasonable request if we humbly desire that it may receive a Christian, charitable, sedate consideration before it be condemned. May we be convinced of any thing therein not agreeable unto the Scriptures, not taught and revealed in them, we shall be with the first in its rejection. That this hath been by any as yet attempted we know not; and yet we are judged, censured, and reproached upon the account of it! So far are men degenerated from that frame of spirit which was in the Christians of old,—so far have they relinquished the ways wherein they walked towards those who dissented from them.

Nor do we decline the judgment of *the primitive church*, being fully satisfied that what we teach and adhere unto is as consonant unto the doctrine thereof as that of any church at this day in the world. The first four general councils, as to what was determined in them in matters of faith, are confirmed by law in this nation; which is all that from antiquity hath any peculiar stamp of authority put upon it amongst us: this also we willingly admit of, and fully assert in our confession. Neither doth the addition of ours disturb the harmony that is in the confessions of the reformed churches, being in all material points the same with them, and no otherwise differing from any of them in things of less importance than as they do one from another, and as all confessions have done, since the first introduction of their use into the churches of God. That which amongst them is of most special regard and consideration unto us, is that of the church of England, declared in the articles of religion; and herein, in particular, what is purely *doctrinal* we fully embrace and constantly adhere unto. And though we shall not compare ourselves with others in ability to assert, teach, and maintain it, yet we cannot, whilst we are conscious unto ourselves of our integrity in our cordial adherence unto it, but hear with regret the clamorous accusations of some against us for departing from the church of England, who have not given that testimony of their adherence unto its doctrine, which we have done, and, by the help of God, shall continue to do. It is true, indeed, there are some enlargements in our confession of the things delivered in the Thirty-nine Articles, some additions of things not expressly contained in them, which we were necessitated unto for the full declaration of our minds, and to obviate that obloquy which otherwise we might have been exposed unto, as reserving our judgment in matters that had received great public debate since the composure of those articles; but yet we are fully persuaded that there is not any proposition in our whole confession which is repugnant unto any thing contained in the articles, or is not by just consequence deducible from them. Neither were we the authors of the explanations or enlargements mentioned, there being nothing contained in them but what we have learned and been instructed in from the writings of the most famous divines of this nation, bishops and others, ever since the Reformation; which being published by legal authority, have been always esteemed, both at home and abroad, faithfully to represent the doctrine of the church of England. We have no new faith to declare, no new doctrine to teach, no private opinions to divulge, no point or truth do we profess, no not one, which hath not been declared, taught, divulged, and esteemed as the common doctrine of the church of England, ever since the Reformation.

If, then, we evince not the faith we profess to be consonant unto the Scriptures, the doctrine of the primitive church of the first four general councils, the confessions of the reformed churches beyond the seas, and that in particular of the church of England, we shall acknowledge the condition of things in reference unto that liberty which we humbly desire to be otherwise stated than hitherto we have apprehended. But if this be the condition of our profession,—as we hope it is manifest unto all unprejudiced and ingenuous persons to be, who esteem it their duty not to judge a matter of so great importance before they hear it,—we can hardly think that they give up themselves to the conduct of the meek and holy Spirit of Christ who are ready to breathe out extirpation against us, as to our interest in this world, for the profession of those principles in the things of God which they pretend to build their own interests upon for another.[1]

---

[1] John Owen, *A Peace-Offering*, in *An Apology and Humble Plea for Indulgence and Liberty of Conscience*, in *Works*, 13:551-52.

Conclusion: John Owen on Confessionalism

Appendix

Outline of the Second London Confession of Faith

I. **First Principles (Chapters 1-6)**
   A. The Scriptures (Chapter 1)
   B. The Doctrine of God (Chapters 2-3)
      1. God's Nature
      2. God's Decree
   C. Creation (Chapters 4-6)
      1. Creation
      2. Providence
      3. Sin

II. **The Covenant (Chapters 7-20)**
   A. The Covenant Defined (Chapter 7)
   B. The Covenant Servant: Christ the Mediator (Chapter 8)
   C. The Covenantal Setting: Free Will (Man's will as created; fallen — in need of covenantal grace; renewed — exercising covenantal grace; and perfected) (Chapter 9)
   D. The Covenant Blessings (God's Acts) (Chapters 10-13)
      1. Effectual Calling
      2. Justification
      3. Adoption
      4. Sanctification

- E. The Covenant Graces (Man's Acts) (Chapters 14-18)
    1. Faith (14.2 — Covenant of Grace)
    2. Repentance (15.2 & 5 — Covenant of Grace)
    3. Good Works
    4. Perseverance (17.2 — Covenant of Grace)
    5. Assurance
- F. The Means of Receiving the Covenant (Chapters 19-20)
    1. God's Law (19.6, 2x — not under a Covenant of Works)
    2. God's Gospel (20.1 — Covenant of Works broken)

III. God-centered Living: Freedom and Boundaries (Chapters 21-30)

- A. The Basis: Liberty of Conscience (Chapter 21)
- B. Principles
    1. The Worship of God (Chapters 22-23)
        a. The Practice of Worship
        b. The Day of Worship
        c. Vows
    2. Civil Government (Chapter 24)
    3. Marriage (Chapter 25)
    4. The Church (Chapters 26-30)

       a. Universal
       b. Local
       c. Fellowship
       d. Sacraments

IV. The World to Come (Chapters 31-32)
   A. The Intermediate and Resurrection States
   B. The Last Judgment

For Reading and Reference

1. *Sine Qua Non*

Muller, Richard A. *Dictionary of Latin and Greek Theological Terms Drawn Principally from Protestant Scholastic Theology*. Second Edition. Grand Rapids: Baker Academic, 2017.
_____. *Post-Reformation Reformed Dogmatics*. Four volumes. Grand Rapids: Baker Academic, 2003.

2. Confessions of Faith/Original Documents

Beeke, Joel R. and Sinclair Ferguson, editors. *Reformed Confessions Harmonized*. Grand Rapids: Baker, 1999.
Collins, Hercules. *An Orthodox Catechism*. Edited by Michael A. G. Haykin and G. Stephen Weaver, Jr. Palmdale, CA: RBAP, 2014.
Dennison, James T., Jr., compiler. *Reformed Confessions of the 16th and 17th Centuries in English Translation*. Four volumes. Grand Rapids: Reformation Heritage Books, 2008-14.
George, Timothy and Denise, editors. *Baptist Confessions, Covenants, and Catechisms*. Nashville: Broadman & Holman, 1996.
Grace Baptist Assembly, *We Believe: The Baptist Affirmation of Faith 1966 & A Guide for Church Fellowship*. London: Grace Baptist Assembly, 1996 reprint.

Lumpkin, William. *Baptist Confessions of Faith*. Valley Forge, PA: Judson Press, 1969 revised edition.

Nettles, Tom J. *Teaching Truths, Training Hearts*. Amityville, NY: Calvary Press, 1998.

Renihan, James M. *Faith and Life for Baptists: The Documents of the London Particular Baptist General Assemblies, 1689-1694*. Palmdale, CA: RBAP, 2016.

Renihan, James M., editor. *True Confessions: Baptist Documents in the Reformed Family*. Owensboro, KY: RBAP, 2004.

Schaff, Philip, editor. *The Creeds of Christendom*. Grand Rapids: Baker Books, 1983 reprint.

Tappert, Theodore G., editor. *The Book of Concord*. Philadelphia: Fortress Press, 1959.

The Baptist Confession of Faith & The Baptist Catechism. Birmingham, AL and Carlisle, PA: Solid Ground Christian Books and Reformed Baptist Publications, 2010.

The Book of Confessions. Philadelphia: The Office of the General Assembly of the United Presbyterian Church in the United States of America, 1967.

The Westminster Standards. Audubon, NJ: Old Paths, 1997 facsimile reprint of 1648 edition.

Underhill, Edward Bean. *Confessions of Faith and other Public Documents, Illustrative of the History of the Baptist Churches of England in the 17th Century*. London: Haddon, Brothers and Co. 1854.

Walker, Williston. *The Creeds and Platforms of Congregationalism*. New York: The Pilgrim Press, 1991.

3. Confessional Subscription

Hall, David W., editor. *The Practice of Confessional Subscription*. Lanham, MD: University Press of America, 1995.

Skilton, John, editor. *Scripture and Confession*. Phillipsburg, PA: Presbyterian and Reformed, 1973.

Smith, Morton. *The Subscription Debate*. Greenville, SC: Greenville Presbyterian Theological Seminary, n.d.

Trueman, Carl. *The Creedal Imperative*. Wheaton: Crossway, 2012.

4. Commentaries/Expositions

Beddome, Benjamin. *A Scriptural Exposition of the Baptist Catechism*. Birmingham, AL: Solid Ground Christian Books, 2006 reprint.

Bethune, George. *Guilt, Grace and Gratitude: Lectures on the Heidelberg Catechism*. Edinburgh: The Banner of Truth Trust facsimile reprint, 2001.

Boston, Thomas. *Commentary on the Shorter Catechism*. Edmonton: Still Waters Revival Books, 1993 reprint of 1853 edition.

Brown, John (Haddington). *Essay Towards an Easy, Plain, Practical and Extensive Explication of the*

Assembly's Shorter Catechism. 1859, from the sixth Edinburgh edition.

Dickson, David. *Truth's Victory over Error*. Edinburgh: Banner of Truth, 2007 reprint.

Erskine, Ebenezer, Ralph Erskine, and James Fisher. *The Shorter Catechism Explained*. Glasgow: n.p., 1765.

Fesko, J. V. *The Theology of the Westminster Standards: Historical Context & Theological Insights*. Wheaton: Crossway, 2014.

Fisher, James. *The Assembly's Shorter Catechism Explained*. Stoke-on-Trent, UK: Berith Publications, 1998 reprint.

Flavel, John. *An Exposition of the Assembly's Shorter Catechism, with Practical Inferences from each Question*, in *The Complete Works of John Flavel*, 6:138-317. London: The Banner of Truth Trust, 1968 reprint.

Goodsir, Joseph Taylor. *The Westminster Confession of Faith examined on the basis of the other Protestant confessions*. London: Williams and Norgate, 1868.

Hodge, Archibald A. *A Commentary on the Confession of Faith*. Edinburgh: The Banner of Truth Trust, 1958 reprint.

Horton, Michael. *We Believe: Recovering the Essentials of the Apostles' Creed*. Nashville: Word, 1998.

MacDonald, James A. *Wesley's Revision of the Shorter Catechism with Notes*. Edinburgh: Geo. Morton, 1906.

MacPherson, John. *The Westminster Confession of Faith with Introduction and Notes*. Edinburgh: T&T Clark, n.d.

Morris, Edward D. *Theology of the Westminster Symbols: A Commentary*. Columbus: Champlin Press, 1900.

Olevianus, Caspar. *A Firm Foundation*. Translated and edited by Lyle Bierma. Grand Rapids: Baker Books, 1995.

Pearson, John. *An Exposition of the Creed*. Oxford: The Clarendon Press, 1877 reprint of 1683 fifth edition.

Perkins, William. *An Exposition of the Symbole or Creede of the Apostles*. Cambridge: John Legat, 1603.

Renihan, James M. *Edification and Beauty: The Practical Ecclesiology of the English Particular Baptists, 1675-1705*. Milton Keynes, UK: Paternoster, 2008.

Ridgely, Thomas. *Commentary on the Larger Catechism*. Two volumes. Edmonton: Still Waters Revival Books, 1993 reprint.

Shaw, Robert. *An Exposition of the Confession of Faith of the Westminster Assembly of Divines*. Glasgow: Blackie and Son, 1857.

Ursinus, Zachary. *The Commentary of Dr. Zachary Ursinus on the Heidelberg Catechism*. Cincinnati: T. P. Bucher, 1851.

Van Dixhoorn, Chad. *Confessing the Faith: A reader's guide to the Westminster Confession of Faith*. Edinburgh: The Banner of Truth Trust, 2014.

Vincent, Thomas. *The Shorter Catechism Explained from Scripture*. Edinburgh: The Banner of Truth Trust, 1980 reprint.

Waldron, Samuel E. *A Modern Exposition of the 1689 Baptist Confession of Faith*. Darlington, UK: Evangelical Press, 1989 (fifth edition 2016).

Wallace, O. C. S. *What Baptists Believe: The New Hampshire Confession: an Exposition*. Nashville: Sunday School Board, 1934.

Ward, Rowland S. *The Westminster Confession for the church today: a modernised text and commentary commemorating the 350th anniversary of the Westminster Assembly 1643-49*. Melbourne: Presbyterian Church of Eastern Australia, 1992.

Watson, Thomas. *A Body of Divinity*. Edinburgh: The Banner of Truth Trust, 1983 reprint.

Westcott, Brooke Foss. *The Historic Faith: Short Lectures on the Apostles' Creed*. London: MacMillan, 1904.

Williamson, G. I. *The Shorter Catechism*. Phillipsburg, NJ: Presbyterian and Reformed, 1970.

_____. *The Westminster Confession of Faith for Study Classes*. Nutley, NJ: Presbyterian and Reformed, n.d.

Witsius, Herman. *Sacred Disputations on the Apostles' Creed*. Escondido, CA: The den Dulk Foundation, 1993 facsimile reprint of Edinburgh: A. Fullarton, 1823.

5. Reformation and Post-Reformation Systematic Theologies

Ames, William. *The Marrow of Theology*. Translated by John Dykstra Eusden. Durham, NC: Labyrinth Press, 1983.

Beza, Theodore. *The Christian Faith*. Translated by James Clark, M.A. Lewes, East Sussex, UK: Focus Christian Ministries Trust, 1992.

Bullinger, Heinrich. *The Decades of Heinrich Bullinger*. Four volumes. Translated in 1587. Cambridge: Parker Translation Society, 1852; reprint, New York: Johnson Reprint Corp., 1968.

Calvin, John. *Institutes of the Christian Religion*. Two volumes. Translated by Ford Lewis Battles. Edited by John T. McNeil. Philadelphia: Westminster Press, 1960.

Leigh, Edward. *A Systeme or Body of Divinity*. London: Printed by A.M., 1654.

Perkins, William. *A Golden Chaine: or, The Description of Theologie*. Cambridge: John Legat, 1603; N.P.: Puritan Reprints, 2010.

Pictet, Benedict. *Christian Theology*. N.P. Forgotten Books, n.d.

Turretin, Francis. *Institutes of Elenctic Theology*. Translated by George Musgrave Giger. Edited by James T. Dennison, Jr. Three volumes. Phillipsburg, NJ: Presbyterian and Reformed, 1994.

Ussher, James. *A Body of Divinity*. Birmingham, AL: Solid Ground Christian Books, 2007 reprint.

Voetius, Gisbert. *Selectae Disputationes Theologicae*, in *Reformed Dogmatics*. Edited by John Beardslee. New York: OUP, 1965, 264-334.

Witsius, Herman. *The Apostles Creed*. Two volumes. Philipsburg, NJ: Presbyterian and Reformed, 1993 reprint.

Wollebius, Johannes. *Compendiom Theologiae Christiane*, in *Reformed Dogmatics*. Edited by John Beardslee. New York, OUP, 1965, 29-262.

6. Books and Articles on Specific Chapters

The following section of the bibliography includes both primary (sixteenth through eighteenth century) and secondary (more recent) sources. I have tried only to include sources available to the modern reader, though occasionally a source is so helpful that it deserves inclusion, even if difficult to find. Books that have been out of print for decades or even centuries are increasingly available through resources such as the *Westminster Assembly Project* (http://www.westminsterassembly.org/assembly-member-works/), the *Post-Reformation Digital Library* (www.prdl.org), Google Books, Archive.org, and Early English Books Online (often accessible through university libraries). In some cases, the literature is vast, and it is assumed that the reader is familiar with standard Puritan works. This work is suggestive rather than exhaustive. An * following the author's name denotes a seventeenth-century Particular Baptist author.

Chapter 1 *Of the Holy Scriptures*

Barcellos, Richard C. "*Scopus Scripturae*: John Owen, Nehemiah Coxe, our Lord Jesus Christ, and a Few Early Disciples on Christ as the Scope of Scripture." *Journal of the Institute of Reformed Baptist Studies* (2015): 5-24.

Brash, Richard Fraser. "The Reformed Doctrine of the Providential Preservation of Scripture, 1588-1687." Unpublished Master of Theology thesis, Westminster Theological Seminary, 2017.

Bridge, William. "Scripture Light the Most Sure Light," in *The Works of the Reverend William Bridge*. Beaver Falls, PA: Soli Deo Gloria, 1989 reprint, 1:401-462.

Frost, R. J. J. "The Doctrine of scripture and the providence of God." Unpublished *Magister Artium* thesis, North-West University, 2014.

Martin, Robert P. "The Second London Confession on the Doctrine of Scripture (Part 1)." *Reformed Baptist Theological Review* IV:1 (January 2007): 59-90; (Part 2) IV:2 (July 2007): 79-126; (Part 3) V:1 (July 2008): 65-91; and (Part IV) VI:1 (Spring 2009): 59-86.

McGraw, Ryan M. *By Good and Necessary Consequence*. Grand Rapids: Reformation Heritage Books, 2012.

Nettles, Tom J. and L. Russ Bush, *Baptists and the Bible*. Chicago: Moody Press, 1980, Chapters 2 and 3, pages 47-72.

Renihan, James. "'Good and Necessary Consequences' or 'Necessarily Contained': A

Particular Baptist Method of Theology" in Richard C. Barcellos, editor. *Southern California Reformed Baptist Pastors' Conference Papers*, Vol. 1, 2012. Palmdale: RBAP, 2012.

_____. "Theology on Target: The Scope of the Whole." *Reformed Baptist Theological Review* II:2 (January 2005): 36-53.

_____. "Sufficient, Certain and Infallible: The Inscripturated Word." *Journal of the Institute of Reformed Baptist Studies* (2015) 43-62.

Renihan, Samuel. "The Consequences of Positive Law: The Particular Baptists' Use of Inferential Reasoning in Theology." *Journal of the Institute of Reformed Baptist Studies* (2016): 123-52.

Warfield, B. B. "The Westminster Doctrine of Holy Scripture," in *The Works of Benjamin B. Warfield*. Volume 6. *The Westminster Assembly and its Work*. Grand Rapids: Baker Book House, 1981 reprint of 1931 OUP edition, 155-257.

Whitaker, William. *Disputations on Holy Scripture*. Orlando: Soli Gloria, 2005 reprint.

Chapter 2 *Of God and the Holy Trinity*

Arnold, Jonathan. *The Reformed Theology of Benjamin Keach (1640-1704)*. Oxford: Regent's Park College, 2013. See chapter 4 "The Godhead," 80-120.

Baines, Ronald S., Richard C. Barcellos, James P. Butler, Stefan T. Lindblad and James M. Renihan, editors. *Confessing the Impassible God:*

The Biblical, Classical, & Confessional Doctrine of Divine Impassibility. Palmdale, CA: RBAP, 2015.

Dolezal, James E. *All That Is in God: Evangelical Theology and the Challenge of Classical Christian Theism*. Grand Rapids, MI: Reformation Heritage Books, 2017.

_____. "Eternal Creator of Time." *Journal of the Institute of Reformed Baptist Studies* (2015): 127-58.

_____. *God without Parts: Divine Simplicity and the Metaphysics of God's Absoluteness*. Eugene, OR: Pickwick, 2011.

_____. "Still Impassible: Confessing God Without Passions." *Journal of the Institute of Reformed Baptist Studies* (2014): 125-52.

Leahy, Frederick. "Does God Suffer?" *The Banner of Truth* 403 (April 1997): 10-17.

Lindblad, Stefan T. "'Eternally Begotten of the Father': An Analysis of the Second London Confession of Faith's Doctrine of the Eternal Generation of the Son," in Ronald S. Baines, Richard C. Barcellos, and James P. Butler, editors. *By Common Confession: Essays in Honor of James M. Renihan*. Palmdale, CA: RBAP, 2015.

_____. "Of the Nature of God: The Inter-Relation of Essence and Trinity in Edward Leigh's A Systeme or Body of Divinity (1662)." *Journal of the Institute of Reformed Baptist Studies* (2014): 95-124.

Owen, Paul. "Calvin and Catholic Trinitarianism: An Examination of Robert Reymond's Understanding of the Trinity and His Appeal to

John Calvin." *Calvin Theological Journal* 35:2 (November 2000): 262-81.

Renihan, Samuel. *God Without Passions: A Primer*. Palmdale, CA: RBAP, 2015.

———. *God Without Passions: A Reader*. Palmdale, CA: RBAP, 2015.

Chapter 3 *Of God's Decree*

Collins, Hercules*. *Mountains of Brass, or A Discourse upon the Decrees of God*. London: John Harris, 1690.

Fesko, John V. *Death in Adam, Life in Christ: The Doctrine of Imputation*. Fearn: Mentor, 2016.

Letham, Robert. *The Westminster Assembly: Reading its Theology in Historical Context*. Phillipsburg: P&R, 2009. See pages 174-88.

Warfield, B. B. "The Making of the Westminster Confession, and Especially of its Chapter on the Decree of God," in *The Works of Benjamin B. Warfield*. Volume 6. *The Westminster Assembly and its Work*. Grand Rapids: Baker Books, 1981 reprint of 1931 OUP edition.

Chapter 4 *Of Creation*

Barcellos, Richard C. *Better Than the Beginning: Creation in Biblical Perspective*. Palmdale, CA: RBAP, 2013.

———. *God plus the World: Confessing the Doctrine of Trinitarian Creation – Accounting for the Confessional Formulation of Creation by our Triune God*. (Forthcoming).

_____. *The Covenant of Works: Its Confessional and Scriptural Basis*. Palmdale, CA: RBAP, 2016.

Flavel, John. *Pneumatologia: A Treatise of the Soul of Man*, in *The Works of John Flavel*. Edinburgh: Banner of Truth, 1982 reprint, 2:475-609, 3:1-238.

Hall, David W. "What was the View of the Westminster Assembly Divines on Creation Days?," in Joseph A. Pipa, Jr., editor. *Did God Create in Six Days?* White Hall, WV: Tolle Lege Press, 1999, 43-54.

Reynolds, Edward. *A Treatise of the Passions and Faculties of the Soul of Man*, in *The Whole Works of the Right Rev. Edward Reynolds*. Ligonier, PA: Soli Deo Gloria, 1992 reprint, 6:1-340.

Chapter 5 *Of Divine Providence*

Ames, William. *The Marrow of Sacred Divinity*. London: Edward Griffin, 1639, 45ff.

Flavel, John. *Divine Conduct, or The Mystery of Providence* in *The Works of John Flavel*. Edinburgh: The Banner of Truth Trust, 1982 reprint, 4:336-497.

Chapter 6 *Of the Fall of Man, of Sin, and of the Punishment thereof*

Coxe, Nehemiah*. *Vindiciae Veritatis, or A Confutation of the Heresies and Gross Errours Asserted by Thomas Collier*. London: Nathaniel Ponder, 1677.

Letham, Robert. *The Westminster Assembly: Reading its Theology in Historical Context*. Phillipsburg: P&R, 2009. See pages 201ff.

Reynolds, Edward. *The Sinfulness of Sin,* in *The Whole Works of the Right Rev. Edward Reynolds*. Ligonier, PA: Soli Deo Gloria, 1992 reprint, 1:102-353.

Chapter 7 *Of God's Covenant*

Barcellos, Richard. C. *Getting the Garden Right: Adam's Work and God's Rest in light of Christ*. Cape Coral, FL: Founders Press, 2017. See especially chapters 1-5.

Barcellos, Richard C. editor. *Recovering a Covenantal Heritage: Essays in Baptist Covenant Theology*. Palmdale, CA: RBAP, 2014. See especially chapters 1-3 and 6-7.

Denault, Pascal. *The Distinctiveness of Baptist Covenant Theology*. Birmingham, AL: Solid Ground Christian Books, 2013.

Coxe, Nehemiah*. *A Discourse of the Covenants*. London: Nathaniel Ponder, 1681.

Fesko, John V. *The Trinity and the Covenant of Redemption*. Fearn: Mentor, 2016.

Hicks, Thomas E. "John Owen on the Mosaic Covenant." *Reformed Baptist Theological Review* VI:1 (Spring 2009): 44-58.

Keach, Benjamin*. *The Display of Glorious Grace: or, The Covenant of Peace Opened*. London: S. Bridge, 1698.

Owen, John. *Hebrews*, Edinburgh: The Banner of Truth Trust, 1991 reprint, 6:49-177.

Renihan, Samuel. "'Dolphins in the Woods': A Critique of Mark Jones and Ted Van Raalte's Presentation of Particular Baptist Covenant

Theology." *Journal of the Institute of Reformed Baptist Studies* (2015): 63-89.

_____. *From Shadow to Substance: The Federal Theology of the English Particular Baptists (1642-1704)*. Oxford: Regent's Park College, Center for Baptist History and Heritage, 2018.

Rollock, Robert. *A Treatise of God's Effectual Calling*. London: Felix Kingston, 1603.

Witsius, Herman. *The Economy of the Covenants between God and Man*. Two volumes. Escondido, CA: Den Dulk Foundation, 1990 reprint.

Woolsey, Andrew A. *Unity and Continuity in Covenantal Thought: A Study in the Reformed Tradition to the Westminster Assembly*. Grand Rapids: Reformation Heritage Books, 2012.

Chapter 8 *Of Christ the Mediator*

Flavel, John. *The Fountain of Life: A Display of Christ in His Essential and Mediatorial Glory*, in *The Works of John Flavel*. Edinburgh: The Banner of Truth Trust, 1982 reprint, 1:17-561.

Owen, John. *CRISTOLOGIA: Or, a Declaration of the Glorious Mystery of the Person of Christ* and *Meditations and Discourses on the Glory of Christ* and *Two Short Catechisms*, in *The Works of John Owen*. Edinburgh: The Banner of Truth Trust, 1981 reprint, 1:1-494.

Chapter 9 *Of Free Will*

Helm, Paul. "Or to Prepare Himself Thereunto." *The Banner of Truth* 175 (April 1978): 20-22.

Luther, Martin. *The Bondage of the Will*. Translated by J. I. Packer and O. R. Johnston. Grand Rapids: Baker Books, 2012.

Chapter 10 *Of Effectual Calling*

Rollock, Robert. *A Treatise of God's Effectual Calling*. London: Felix Kingston, 1603.

Chapter 11 *Of Justification*

Arnold, Jonathan, *The Reformed Theology of Benjamin Keach*. See chapter 6, 160-201.

Goodwin, Thomas. *Works*. Volume 8. Edinburgh: The Banner of Truth Trust, 1985 reprint.

Hicks, Tom. "Popery in New Dress: Richard Baxter v. Benjamin Keach on the Doctrine of Justification," in *By Common Confession*, 73-102.

Keach, Benjamin*. *The Marrow of True Justification*. London: Newman, 1692.

Keach, Elias*. *A Plain and Familiar Discourse on Justification*. London: John Harris, 1694.

Machen, J. G. *God Transcendent*. Grand Rapids: Eerdmans, 1949, 190-91.

Owen, John. *The Doctrine of Justification by Faith*, in *Works*, 6:1-400.

Renihan, James M. "Reforming the Reformed Pastor: Baptism and Justification as the basis for Richard Baxter's Pastoral Method." *Reformed Baptist Theological Review* II:1 (January 2005): 111-34.

Walker, Austin. "Benjamin Keach and the 'Baxterian' Controversy of the 1690s." *Reformed*

Baptist Theological Review III:1 (January 2006): 3-26.

Chapter 12 *Of Adoption*
Beeke, Joel, *Heirs with Christ: The Puritans on Adoption*. Grand Rapids: Reformation Heritage Books, 2008.

———. "Transforming Power and Comfort: The Puritans on Adoption" http://www.reclaimingthemind.org/papers/ets/2005/beeke/beeke.pdf.

Chapter 13 *Of Sanctification*
Burroughs, Jeremiah. *Gospel Conversation*. Morgan, PA: Soli Deo Gloria, 1995 reprint.

Marshall, Walter. *The Gospel Mystery of Sanctification*. Welwyn: Evangelical Press, 1981 reprint.

Chapter 14 *Of Saving Faith*
Flavel, John. *The Method of Grace,* in *The Works of John Flavel*. Edinburgh: The Banner of Truth Trust, 1982 reprint, 2:1-474.

Renihan, James M. "The Increase of Faith: The Ordinary Means of Grace in the Second London Confession of Faith." *Reformed Baptist Theological Review* I:2 (July 2004): 74-94.

Chapter 15 *Of Repentance unto Life and Salvation*
Blackwood, Christopher*. *A Treatise concerning Repentance*. London: Giles Calvert, 1653.

Watson, Thomas. *The Doctrine of Repentance, Useful for these Times*. London: R.W. 1668.

Chapter 16 *Of Good Works*

Owen, John. *Hebrews*, 7:284ff.

Polanus, Amandus. *The Substance of Christian Religion, soundly set forth in two Bookes, . . . the First Booke concerneth faith. The second concerneth good works*. London: R.F. 1597.

Preston, John. *The Breast-plate of Faith and Love*. Edinburgh: The Banner of Truth Trust facsimile reprint, 1979.

Chapter 17 *Of the Perseverance of the Saints*

Owen, John. *The Doctrine of the Saints Perseverance Explained and Confirmed,* in *Works*, 11:1-666.

Turretin, Francis. *Institutes of Elenctic Theolog*, 1:569.

Chapter 18 *Of the Assurance of Grace and Salvation*

Beeke, Joel R.. *Assurance of Faith: Calvin, English Puritanism, and the Dutch Second Reformation*. New York: Peter Lang, 1994.

_____. "Personal Assurance of Faith: The Puritans and Chapter 18.2 of the Westminster Confession." *Westminster Theological Journal* 55 (Spring 1993): 1-30.

_____. "Understanding Assurance." *Banner of Truth* 392 (May 1996): 16-21; 394 (July 1996): 9-17.

Guthrie, William. *The Christian's Great Interest*. Edinburgh: The Banner of Truth Trust, 1969 reprint.

Helm, Paul. *Calvin and the Calvinists*. Edinburgh: The Banner of Truth Trust, 1982, 23-31.

Owen, John. *Gospel Grounds and Evidences of the Faith of God's Elect*, in *Works*, 5:401-57.

Chapter 19 *Of the Law of God*

Barcellos, Richard C. "How the 'uses of the law . . . sweetly comply with . . . the grace of the Gospel' (2LCF 19.7), 2016 ARBCA Circular Letter. http://s3.amazonaws.com/churchplantmedia-cms/arbca_carlisle_pa/2016-arbca-circular-letter-2.pdf.

Burgess, Anthony. *Vindiciae Legis, or A Vindication of the Morall Law and the Covenants . . .* London: Thomas Underhill, 1647. http://www.westminsterassembly.org/wp-content/uploads/Burgess-Vindiceae-text-complete.pdf.

Casselli, Steven J. *Divine Rule Maintained: Anthony Burgess, Covenant Theology, and the Place of the Law in Reformed Scholasticism*. Grand Rapids: Reformation Heritage Books, 2016.

Kevan, Ernest. *The Grace of Law*. Grand Rapids: Baker Books, 1976.

Chapter 20 *Of the Gospel, and of the Extent of the Grace Thereof*

Owen, John. *Biblical Theology*. Translated by Stephen Westcott. Pittsburgh: Soli Deo Gloria, 1994. Book 1, chapter 6, page 44ff.

———. *Exposition of Hebrews*. Edinburgh: The Banner of Truth Trust, 22:70.

———. *A Vision of Unchangeable, Free Mercy, In Sending The Means Of Grace To Undeserving Sinners*, in *Works*, 8:1ff.

Renihan, James M. "Church Planting and the London Baptist Confessions of Faith." *Founders Journal* 37 (Summer 1999): 10-19.

———. "'That Stronghold of Their Common Faith': Salvation in Christ Alone among Seventeenth Century Baptists." *Journal of the Institute of Reformed Baptist Studies* (2014): 69-94.

Chapter 21 *Of Christian Liberty and Liberty of Conscience*

Bolton, Samuel. *The True Bounds of Christian Freedom*. London: J.L., 1645. A slightly edited version has been published by The Banner of Truth Trust in their Puritan Paperbacks series.

Calvin, John. *Institutes*. Book 3, chapter 19.

Danvers, Henry*. *Certain Quaeries concerning Liberty of Conscience*. London: Giles Calvert, 1649.

De Laune, Thomas*. *A Plea for the Non-Conformists*. London: Printed for the Author, 1684.

———. *Compulsion of Conscience Condemned*. London: John How, 1683.

Downame, George. *The Christian's Freedom*. Pittsburgh: Soli Doe Gloria, 1994 reprint.

Owen, John. *Works*, 13:402.

Chapter 22 *Of Religious Worship and the Sabbath Day*

Barcellos, Richard. C. *Getting the Garden Right: Adam's Work and God's Rest in light of Christ*. Cape Coral, FL: Founders Press, 2017. See especially chapters 6-14.

Keach, Benjamin*. *The Breach Repaired in God's Worship*. London: John Hancock, 1691.

———. *The Jewish Sabbath Abrogated: or, the Saturday Sabbatarians Confuted*. London: John Marshall, 1700.

Lindblad, Donald R. "New Covenant Worship: Hebrews 2:12 and the Real Presence of Christ," in *By Common Confession*, 409-44.

Renihan, James M. "'Bound to Keep the First Day': Covenant Theology, the Moral Law, and the Sabbath among the First English Particular Baptists." *Reformed Baptist Theological Review* III:2 (July 2006): 51-76.

Waldron, Samuel E. "The Regulative Principle of the Church," in *By Common Confession*, 377-408.

———. "The Regulative Principle of Worship: Contemporary Objections." *Journal of the Institute of Reformed Baptist Studies* (2016): 185-215.

Chapter 23 *Of Lawful Oaths and Vows*

Burgess, Anthony. *Vindiciae Legis, or A Vindication of the Morall Law and the Covenants . . .* London: Thomas Underhill, 1647. http://www.westminsterassembly.org/wp-content/uploads/Burgess-Vindiceae-text-complete.pdf. See page 185.

Musculus, Wolfgang. *On Righteousness, Oaths, and Usury.* Grand Rapids: Acton Institute, 2013.

Chapter 24 *Of the Civil Magistrate*

Baines, Ronald S. "Separating God's Two Kingdoms: Two Kingdom Theology among New England Baptists in the Early Republic." *Journal of the Institute of Reformed Baptist Studies* (2014): 27-68.

Harrison, Edward*. *Plain Dealing . . . Wherein is set down, the Rise, Nature and Species of Right Government.* London: J. Harris, 1649.

Owen, John. *Works*, 13:507-592. This section of the reprint of Owen's writings contains several brief tracts written to address the rights of church and state.

Chapter 25 *Of Marriage*

Gouge, William. *Of Domesticall Duties.* London: Iohn Haviland, 1622.

Owen, John. *Of Marrying after Divorce in the Case of Adultery*, in *Works*, 16:254-57.

Presbyterian Church of America position paper on Divorce and Remarriage: http://www.pcahistory.org/pca/divorce-remarriage.pdf. This has a helpful bibliography of relevant confessional writings beginning on page 199.

Chapter 26 *Of the Church*

Brown, Michael. "Occasional Conformity: The Congregationalism of Henry Jacob and John Owen." *Reformed Baptist Theological Review* VI:1 (Spring 2009): 87-106.

Cotton, John. "The Keys of the Kingdom of Heaven," in *John Cotton on the Churches of New England*. Edited by Larzer Ziff. Belknap Press, 1968, pages 71-164.

Coxe, Nehemiah*. *A Sermon Preached at the Ordination of an Elder and Deacons in a Baptized Congregation in London*. London: Tho. Fabian, 1681. Reprinted in *Reformed Baptist Theological Review* I:1 (January 2004): 133-56.

Goodwin, Thomas. *Works*, 11:484-546. All of volume 11 is relevant.

Keach, Benjamin*. *The Glory of a True Church, and its Discipline Display'd*. London: n.p., 1697.

Kiffin, William*. *A Sober Discourse of Right to Church Communion*. London: G. Larkin, 1681.

Owen, John. *Works*, 15:188-373, 446-530; 16:2-208, 223-237, 241-253.

Renihan, James M. *Associational Churchmanship: Second London Confession of Faith 26.12-15*. Palmdale, CA: RBAP, 2016.

_____. "Ecclesiology in Debate: 'Whether Jesus Christ Shall be King or No.'" *Reformed Baptist Theological Review* VII:2 (Fall 2010): 41-72.

_____. *Edification and Beauty*.

Chapter 27 *Of the Communion of Saints*

Keach, Benjamin*. *Exposition of the Parables*. London: Aylott, 1858 Reprint, 56, 150, 300.

Owen, John. *Hebrews*, 4:138-41.

Whately, William. *The Poore Mans Advocate, or, a Treatise of Liberality to the needy*. London: G.M., 1637.

Chapter 28 *Of Baptism and the Lord's Supper*

Crampton, W. Gary. "The Sacramental Implications of 1 Corinthians 10:1-4: A Confessional Study of Baptism and the Lord's Supper." *Reformed Baptist Theological Review* VII:2 (Fall 2010): 7-40.

Chapter 29 *Of Baptism*

Barcellos, Richard C., editor. *Recovering a Covenantal Heritage: Essays in Baptist Covenant Theology*. Palmdale, CA: RBAP, 2014. See especially chapters 4-5.

Martin, Robert P. "The Second London Confession on Baptism." *Reformed Baptist Theological Review* II:1 (January 2005): 36-55.

_____. "The Subjects of Baptism in the Confession." *Reformed Baptist Theological Review* II:2 (July 2005): 54-86; III:1, (January 2006): 48-76.

Chapter 30 *Of the Lord's Supper*

Barcellos, Richard C. "Communion at the Lord's Supper: 1 Corinthians 10:16 in its Exegetical and

Confessional Context." *Journal of the Institute of Reformed Baptist Studies* (2014): 7-26.

_____. *The Lord's Supper as a Means of Grace: More than a Memory*. Fearn, Ross-shire, UK: Mentor, 2013.

Weaver, Jr., G. Stephen. "Christ Spiritually Present and Believers Spiritually Nourished: The Lord's Supper in 17th-Century English Particular Baptist Life." *Journal of the Institute of Reformed Baptist Studies* (2015): 91-126.

Chapter 31 *Of the State of Man after Death, and of the Resurrection of the Dead*

Flavel, John. *The Present and Future State of Christless Souls* in *Works*, 2:422-74.

Knollys, Hanserd*. *Apocalyptical Mysteries*. London: n.p., 1667.

_____. *An Exposition of the Whole Book of the Revelation*. London: William Marshall, 1688.

Toon, Peter, editor. *Puritans, The Millennium and The Future of Israel: Puritan Eschatology 1600 to 1660*. Edinburgh: James Clarke & Co. Ltd., 1970.

Chapter 32 *Of the Last Judgment*

Arnold, Jonathan, *The Reformed Theology of Benjamin Keach*. See chapter 7 "Millenarian Eschatology," 202-45.

Danvers, Henry*. *Theopolis, or the City of God New Jerusalem*. London: T. Ratcliff, 1672.

Gribben, Crawford. *The Puritan Millennium: Literature and Theology, 1550-1682 (Revised Edition)*. Milton Keynes, UK: Paternoster, 2008.

Hill, Christopher. *The Experience of Defeat*. New York: Viking, 1984, 51ff.

Keach. Benjamin*. *Antichrist Stormed*. London: Nathaniel Crouch, 1689.

Toon, Peter, editor. *Puritans, The Millennium and the Future of Israel*. Edinburgh: James & Co., 1970.

Reading and Reference